Young Children Learning

Young Children Learning

Reaching Out

Alice Yardley

Principal Lecturer in Education,
Nottingham College of Education

MEDIA CENTER
CHAPEL HILL CITY SCHOOLS

Citation Press · New York · 1973

Published by Evans Brothers Limited
Montague House, Russell Square, London, W.C.1

Citation Press, Library and Trade Division, Scholastic Magazines, Inc.
50 West 44th St., New York, New York 10036

© Alice Yardley, 1970

All rights reserved. No part of this publication may be reproduced, stored in a retrieval system, or transmitted in any form or by any means, electronic, mechanical, photocopying, recording or otherwise, without the prior permission of Evans Brothers Limited.

The following are the four titles in the
YOUNG CHILDREN LEARNING series by Alice Yardley:

REACHING OUT
EXPLORATION AND LANGUAGE
DISCOVERING THE PHYSICAL WORLD
SENSES AND SENSITIVITY

Also by Alice Yardley:
THE TEACHER OF YOUNG CHILDREN
YOUNG CHILDREN THINKING

Library of Congress Catalog Card Number: 72-95335
Standard Book Number: 590-07328-1

Cover photograph: Henry Grant, AIIP

Printed in Great Britain by T. and A. Constable Ltd.,
Hopetoun Street, Edinburgh.

PRA 3168

Contents

	Author's note	7
	Introduction by Kenneth Baird	9
1	The need to learn	11
2	Learning, living and playing	15
3	The integrated nature of learning	25
4	The pattern of learning	30
5	The individuality of the child	36
6	The developing person	42
7	The importance of environment	49
8	Preparing the environment	55
9	Working together	61
10	The integrated day	68
11	Home and school	77
12	The mental health of the child	84
13	The gifted child and the slow learner	91
14	The teacher and her job	101
	Suggestions for further reading	107
	Index	112

Reference numbers in the text indicate particular books in the Suggestions for further reading.

Author's Note

This book is the first of a series of four in which issues affecting the organisation and work of the modern Infant School are considered. Each book covers a range of topics connected with a particular aspect of the child's life in school. While the ideas expressed in *Reaching Out* provide the foundation on which the other books are based, each book is complete in itself. Some aspects of the work intentionally overlap, and where this occurs the material is considered from different standpoints.

These books are written for parents, for students in colleges of education, for practising teachers and for any others who are interested in the education of young children. Factual examples from classroom situations support the text throughout. The aim generally is to express educational theory in terms of the work of teachers and children.

Many of the views held by teachers today are the outcome of personal experience. Not all of them have been tested and proved by research. Indeed, some findings may appear so obviously true to those who know children well that to prove them by clinical methods would seem unnecessary. Parents and practising teachers have many things to tell the psychologist. Much of what they do is rooted in their intuitive understanding of children and their behaviour. They may not always be able to explain why they apply certain methods, or how they come by their ideas. This does not invalidate their work and beliefs, and the psychologist would be the first to admit that there are no definite answers to many questions associated with the upbringing and education of young children.

Fundamental to these books is a careful examination of the teacher's job, and frequent reference is made to the work she does and the responses she gains from the children. I have, therefore, recorded as simply as possible what I feel to be true about children and I quote extensively from personal experience and from the experience of parents, teachers and children I know well. My first intention is to capture the joy shared by adults and children who are privileged to live and work in the Infant Schools of today.

Many people have helped me to collect and prepare my material and I should like to acknowledge my indebtedness to them. Some gave me help in special ways. José Moss provided material for the chapter on slow-learning and gifted children in *Reaching Out*. Margaret Smith outlined the approach to understanding history and Allen Young to understanding geography in *Discovering the Physical World*. Other specialist colleagues helped to check relevant parts of the text. Douglas Kaye assisted with mathematics and John Tollyfield with science in *Discovering the Physical World*, and Robin Protheroe with divinity and Malcolm Anderton with music in *Senses and Sensitivity*.

At all points in the series I am indebted to Allen Young for his advice on learning theory and research and for his infinite patience in checking the text.

Finally I must record my gratitude to all those children, their parents and their teachers who for many years have shared their experiences so generously with me.

Alice Yardley

Introduction

This is a book about all our children: not about abstract nouns like 'intelligence', but about Peter and John and Jean and Joan. We can recognise them all in Alice Yardley's pages.

The book tells one of the great success stories of our time. The dreariness of our great cities, the complexity of technology, and the ferocity of meritocracy all threaten to destroy our culture, and it sometimes seems as though the only thing to set in the scales opposite them is the great truth grasped by the infant teachers, which outweighs them all. This truth is that to want to learn is far, far more important than to be taught.

Infant teachers have adhered to their inspiration, and they are winning. The odds against them are great. Infant classes are bigger than any other classes, partly because there are so many children and partly because infant teachers are persuaded so soon into marriage; and if the devoted spinster of yesteryear is disappearing, in her place we have more educated mothers than ever before. A married woman has twenty years of constructive living after her children become independent. She can rear a family and then return to teaching, bringing with her ideas which have developed through her own experience of her children. For the infant teacher makes a better mother and a mother can be an excellent and detached infant teacher.

Reaching out

These books are the result of the work of some of my colleagues, but I am sure they would all maintain that it was Alice Yardley who led them and who drove them. For many years she was a highly successful headmistress. She is no abstract theorist. She knows her children, but now I rejoice to say that she knows her students and her colleagues and can spread through them her unquenchable enthusiasm. The tutorial method of a college is very like that of an Infant School, but how few children win through to college, and how many in the years between eleven and twenty-one lose all desire to learn and all excitement in the discovery of the good, the beautiful and the true. This is the waste energy of our society which Alice Yardley and her colleagues know how to harness.

Kenneth A. Baird,
Principal,
Nottingham College of Education

1

The need to learn

The relationship between teacher and child has changed fundamentally during the last thirty years and it is in this field that educational developments can most clearly be seen. The mere physical position of the teacher in the modern Infant School classroom is indicative of significant changes in her concept of her job. She no longer stands isolated, remote from the children, facing them as they sit silently in pairs, awaiting her instruction. She is *amongst* the children, and they are at work in all parts of the classroom. With one eye on, say, certain water experiments, she may be showing Jane how to cast on her knitting, pausing perhaps to write down a word for Peter in his word-book. It may even take an onlooker several minutes to locate her whereabouts in the classroom.

Small groups of children are at work in every available corner of the school, inside and outside the classroom. For much of the time they appear to be independent of adult assistance. Each child chooses his own job and is responsible for it: he has time to finish this before moving on to another. The whole school is his workshop and the equipment he finds in it is there for his use. Within certain limits, he is free to come and go as he chooses. The teacher is there to provide help when he needs it, rather than to instruct and direct his activities.

A foreign visitor, introduced to an Infant School classroom

at half-past nine in the morning, exclaimed: 'Ah! It is playtime already?' Closer observation reveals that what may appear to be confusion, or desultory play, makes sense to the child. He knows his way around and is obviously in charge of his own affairs. He is absorbed in what he is doing. He is *learning* through things which interest him rather than *being taught*. He is the centre of what is happening, and it is his job, and not the teacher's, that demands his attention.

Today, as parents or teachers we take the trouble to get to know our children and to find out what they need to help them to grow as individual people. We expect them to be immature and to learn at their own level. The task of the school is to enable the child to develop his own particular personality as fully as possible. The child's home has already contributed much to his education, but the wider horizon of school and a change of adult influence can extend his opportunities for growth.

Parents and teachers are powerful influences in a child's life. It is very tempting to try to mould a child into a pale image of ourselves, or of what we would like to be. We may even resent the child's individuality when he thwarts us. But, as adults, our main responsibility is to encourage his individuality, accepting him as different from ourselves and from everyone else. We give him credit for knowing better than us where his interests lie.

Work in the schools is based on the nature of the child and our own knowledge about the way in which he develops. During the last fifty years extensive research has provided many facts about the physical, emotional and intellectual growth of the child.[1] There is much we have yet to discover, but we know enough to establish a number of important principles. A consideration of some of these will provide the framework for the pattern of learning established for the child in school.

A study of children learning must start with the baby,

The need to learn

because this is where all learning begins. At birth the human child can cry, suck, breathe and move his limbs, but little more. Practically everything he will ultimately achieve as an adult has to be learned. He has to learn how to co-ordinate his body movements, how to speak, how to get on with other people, how to control and handle his emotions, how to think, and later he has to find himself a philosophy for living. He doesn't learn these things one at a time. We cannot isolate the skill of speech, for instance, from thinking and communicating with others. Learning, for the child, is a complex, co-ordinated experience.

Some creatures, such as ants, inherit patterns of behaviour. Within moments of birth they can fend for themselves. Effective modes of dealing with environmental problems are built-in and thus make them independent of assistance from others. There is little they need to learn and their behaviour has not changed for 50 million years. This technique of survival operates only within rigid patterns of behaviour.

The human baby can do very little. His development will take many years and his learning will be very varied.[2] He scores over the ant by becoming uniquely individual in his behaviour and by accomplishing an infinite variety of skills. Initially he is handicapped by being almost completely helpless and therefore dependent on others. It is because he is helpless that he learns. He strives constantly to achieve what others require of him in order to please and manipulate the people on whom he depends.

As all mothers know, the child is born with a desire, a desperate urge, to learn: he would die if he didn't start to learn pretty quickly. We don't need to persuade the child to learn if we follow his natural inclinations. He must learn and we are there to help him.

Birth is not so much a beginning as an interruption of the developmental pattern. Some babies find the shock too great. Their urge to learn is not strong enough to survive the sudden change from the stable, protected environment of the womb, to the world of changes and independence.

In one Midland hospital doctors could diagnose no physical reason for the inability of a baby to take nourishment and come to terms with the world. He lay limp, his crumpled face peering in misery at a world he found completely unpalatable. There was no urge to live and so it seemed inappropriate to call the baby by a name. After two weeks the baby died, because, in the nurse's terms, 'he just didn't seem to *want* to live'. He lacked the vital drive to survive.

Such cases are rare. The baby's first lusty cry is a demand for air, which from now on will enable him to live an existence independent of his mother. From now on the urge to learn will be an essential factor in his development. He will obey his urge through infancy and bring it with him into the schools.[3]

2

Learning, living and playing

Jane came into school from a 'professional' home. For the first few days she appeared to be happy. Her interest in the book-corner delighted her teacher and Jane showed many signs of being a quick learner. On the fifth day the sound of a child sobbing in the corner attracted the teacher's attention. Much to her surprise she found Jane staring at an open book with huge tears brimming her eyes. Anguished sobs shook her small body beneath the teacher's arm. At length an explanation emerged.

'I can't read,' the child confided. 'Mummy said I would when I came to school and I can't.' Jane was intelligent. She knew that books were important at home and that the miracle of learning to read was expected of her. She saw school as an opportunity to acquire a skill which would qualify her for her appropriate role in the home. Her whole intent was focused on earning the approval of her parents. She would need to learn how to accept and then to overcome her own limitations.

When Mother brought Peter to school she explained to the teacher: 'You'll find Peter a good boy. He's been brought up in a flat and he had to be kept quiet because of the old lady below. I hope he'll make friends now. He's not been used to playing with other children and I think he needs other children to bring him out a bit.'

Reaching out

Peter remained a 'good' boy until he felt safe enough to start exploring. By the end of the week his pent-up energies were seeking violent outlets. Equipment became weapons and materials were missiles. He snatched what he wanted and bit any child who thwarted him. His first freedom had gone to his head. He had no idea how to treat other children.

His teacher tried to develop the interest he showed in woodwork. One day he made a cart and tried to fasten wheels to it, but they wouldn't stay on and so he approached his teacher. 'Can you make the wheels stay on?' he asked her. His teacher seized the opportunity.

'Robin will help you,' she said, 'if you wait until he's finished painting his picture and then ask him properly.' Ten minutes later Peter was holding the wheels while Robin screwed them to the cart. This was his first experience of co-operating with another child. It was the beginning of a stormy friendship and his first attempt to become a social being.

The child in the Infant School behaves in very varied ways. He delights in his skill on the climbing apparatus; he can thread beads; he shows a lively interest in unfamiliar and curious things; he is anxious to find out about his environment and learns to manipulate it; he responds to suggestions made by his teacher, and he may try to resist them; he is anxious to enlist the help of another child; he makes friends quickly and just as quickly he quarrels; he laughs easily and has learned to hold back his tears.

Each of these modes of behaviour represents a form of adjustment, a way in which the child has accommodated himself to a situation or person. He has been striving for five years to understand the world around him and the people in it. He is anxious to learn how he fits into the pattern himself and in five years has accomplished a great deal.

The act of living and developing is a constant process of adjustment between the baby and his environment. But

Learning, living and playing

the human baby is not content with merely adjusting; he strives also to understand his world so that he can master it.

If his world consisted entirely of things, learning about it would be comparatively simple. Things are reasonably constant and what the child discovers about them remains permanent information. The baby chews coal. He pours and splashes the water. He squeezes and pokes and pummels the clay, and so he finds out what these things can do and what he can do with them.

He may at first apply the same principles of discovery to people, but he soon finds that biting and squeezing and poking do not produce the most desirable responses from people. People are much more variable than things. They are much more difficult to understand and consequently much more educative. Eventually, the child discovers that growing up amongst people requires much effort from him. He must make tremendous adjustments if he is to achieve what he most desires, which is the approval of others and the security of their protection.

The amount of adjustment the child makes depends on the extent to which his effort is provoked. The hungry baby is in desperate need of his mother's attention and will exert every effort to attract it. He will call upon all his resources to manipulate her into satisfying his needs.

At birth the human baby is helpless. This means that he is dependent on the people who care for him. He has a set of needs which other people must satisfy. This renders him very sensitive to the influence of others. He must communicate his needs to others and gain their co-operation. He responds to them and this evokes a response towards him. He soon learns that his vocal noises provide him with an effective channel of communication.

The human baby develops slowly. This means he has a long time in which to learn and this in turn enables him to go a long way. A calf can stand within minutes of birth, and within months it has acquired the full range of its movements. It takes months for the baby to reach the walking stage, but the movements of a nine-year-old child provide ample evidence of the very great capacity of the child for physical learning.

During the long process of adjustment to people the child progresses through many stages and we come to expect different modes of behaviour at each one.[4]

We accept the three-year-old with an indulgent smile when he bursts into the room and announces 'I'm here!' A five-year-old, finding a new playmate in school, may relinquish his toy as a gesture of friendship. When he sees the other child beginning to enjoy playing with it he may snatch it back, and we respond by pacifying the victim. We expect the seven-year-old to withhold his demands on our attention when we are dealing with another child who is sick. At each stage we only demand of the child what we have learned to expect of him. We know that the process of becoming a mature person takes twenty-one years, or even longer.

Perhaps the most vigorous stages of the child's learning take place before he enters school. He learns from his family, and the effect his home and family have on him is very clearly seen by the teacher.[5] One of the most interesting areas in an Infant School classroom is the domestic play-corner. The observer here soon knows how a child feels about his parents and what he finds significant in the life of his home.

Domestic play varies tremendously between schools in different neighbourhoods. Watching the house play, for instance, in a school in a down-town area the onlooker invariably notices a male figure lolling about the house or reeling around outside it. House play in a school situated in a better residential area is a very different matter. Here we find perpetual genteel tea-parties and the father figure is rarely part of the game.

The attitudes, beliefs and speech of parents are so thoroughly

Learning, living and playing

conveyed to their children that later education has little effect on them.[6] A child brought up in a Yorkshire home may be educated in a first-class Grammar School and then at Cambridge. His speech may become polished, but get him to relax and you will soon be asking which part of Yorkshire he comes from.

In school the child's friends play a considerable part in the learning process. By the time he is six or seven he wants friends and feels the need to be accepted by other children. As he grows older the acceptance of friends takes precedence over other relationships. He will modify his needs and interests considerably to gain the approval of his group.

Many children find this part of their learning very difficult. They are shy or bossy, selfish or aggressive, self-opinionated or over-demanding. Other children don't want to do all the adjusting and great skill is required of the teacher to help difficult children join in the give and take of forming good relationships.

Pamela at the age of six tended to dominate. The arrival of a baby sister accentuated the problem and the other children in her class began to call her 'Bossy Boots'. Her teacher put her in charge of the distribution of milk, letting her boss the milk bottles and so helping her to be of service to other children. This put her in a position where her friends could help her to regain her confidence in herself as an important and needed person. Things improved.

Children fight. This is one of their ways of getting to know one another and they need to do it. Adults tend to frown on fighting in children and sometimes, of course, it has to be stopped if we are to prevent physical damage. The child's aggression, however, is an important part of his survival equipment. Parents need to recognise this, instead of being ashamed if their children fight. They are afraid of the opinion of others and will go to great lengths to build up attitudes in their children which are quite against the child's nature.

Reaching out

Children exploring human relationships for the first time try a wide range of approaches. They fight easily and make up easily. Their fighting leaves no rancour and is a healthy way for the immature to come to terms with one another. It is all part of the exploration of another person in childhood.

The child's greatest asset in the process of learning is his ability to play.[7] It is through his play that he manages to come to terms with the world and make it something he can understand and control. The child who does not play has no really effective means of developing.

Inside the entrance hall of a residential school for educationally subnormal children stands a huge Wendy House. It is beautifully equipped, and was presented by a benefactor in the hope that it would please the children. Unfortunately it is often empty. The only use these children have for it is as an occasional place to hide away in. The only purpose they have for the toys in it is to use them as missiles. These children do not know how to play. Consequently they have no effective means of learning. Their learning is painfully slow and very erratic. Their problems indicate a very close relationship between intellect and the child's capacity for play. Susan Isaacs reminds us that 'play is supremely the activity which brings the child psychic equilibrium in the early years'.

It is difficult for adults to understand what play means to the child. We have no means of remembering precisely what our own experience was, or what we gained from it. Many adults regard play as a pleasant means of passing the time and sometimes even as a complete waste of it. The busy mother dismisses her child by telling him to 'make himself scarce', or to 'run away and play'. She provides him with things that will keep him quiet, or occupy him so that he will not require her attention.

Many teachers allow for play in the timetable as an 'outlet' or chance to relax from the effort of work, applying the theory

Learning, living and playing

that 'all work and no play makes Jack a dull boy'. They may recognise the fact that it 'does something for the young child', but how many of them really recognise play to be the most essential factor in a child's development? There is still in the minds of many parents and teachers something of the attitude of the father who complained that his child couldn't be learning anything worth while at school because she enjoyed it and liked coming. 'Kids do nothing but play nowadays, and it can't be good for them.'

Many of our great educators have sensed that play is something the child *must* do and that he does it for its own sake. Over 2,000 years ago Plato emphasised the significance of play in the *Laws*. Froebel regarded play as the highest phase of a child's development, the purest and most spiritual aspect of man at this stage. Susan Isaacs, in more recent years, sees in play the child's means of coming to terms with the world, of finding out about himself and of accepting his own limitations and the limitations imposed on him by others.

If children in school are left free to react spontaneously to their materials, definite patterns of play can be observed. In the sand tray, for instance, children will start by experimenting in order to find out what sand will do. Dry sand trickles through the fingers, and feels gritty between them. It sifts through the holes in a sieve, or piles in a cone as it pours through a funnel. These experiments may even extend to watching sand spray out when it is flung across the room, but sand in the hair or the eye is not a pleasing experience and we usually halt children at this point in discovery.

Add water, and sand behaves in a different way. It sticks together and will stay heaped in a pie. A heap of wet sand, squeezed, holds the print of clenched fingers. It can be moulded into mountains and valleys. As the surface dries it begins to sift down and can be blown into ripples.

At this point the sand may be abandoned. Little evidence of what has been learned is observable until, one day, Philip brings his toy cars and returns to the wet sand in order to mould a landscape which provides a realistic situation for his play with cars. Philip knows by now what sand will do for him and how he can make it serve his purpose. He now employs this knowledge, making the sand fulfil the idea he has in his mind.

These principles apply not only to basic materials such as clay, paint, bricks, water, and so on, but also to sounds, words, numbers and other symbols, to equipment and apparatus, and to human relationships. There is first the active exploration of the material, forcing it to reveal its true nature. An internalising period follows this first stage, before the child returns to his material with a purpose in mind. The child will apply this process to most of the materials we offer him, if we leave him to make the discoveries for himself. If we give him materials and tell him what to do with them, he doesn't have the same opportunity for learning.

Adults are often dismayed when children 'play about with materials and make nothing of them'. From the adult point of view the time and the material have been wasted unless the child produces an end-product.

This quiescent stage is in fact the most important phase in the learning process. It is here that knowledge of the material becomes part of the child's mind. Future use of material is a by-product of this learning stage. If we try to hurry the child through the internalising period his learning becomes shallow.

At all stages in human development we approach unfamiliar material in much the same way. As mature people we may pass more quickly through the early part of the process, but effective learning only takes place where we are allowed to experience this stage to the full.

The exploration of human relationships follows a similar pattern. In the early stages the child is preoccupied with the job of getting to know himself as a pattern of what a person is. He plays alone, or alongside another child. In the Nursery

Learning, living and playing

School play is frequently solitary, or parallel. In the Infant School play becomes more social and is the means by which children find out about others.

Stephen collected all the big bricks and started to build a wall. He then decided to enlist the assistance of Ian because he wanted to build 'the longest wall in the world'. Ian followed Stephen's instructions for a time and then had an idea of his own. Ian's idea clashed with Stephen's and a short fight followed. What happened during the fight wasn't clear, but shortly after this Stephen and Ian were working as partners with a gathering crowd of admirers to cheer them on. Through their play each had made adjustments and discovered that more could be achieved together.

The play of children aged five to seven is well developed and takes a number of forms. There is the free exploration of new materials, situations and personal relationships. There is the dramatic play of the domestic corner when the child explores the personality of others by identifying with them.[8] There is the constructive play which takes place with junk and waste materials. There is the therapeutic type of play in which the child plays out his emotions and gets rid of aggression and guilt feelings which often torment him. We know as we watch James pounding the clay and thundering the nails home, or Patricia spanking her dolly, that energies, possibly dangerous ones, are being expended.

We realise, too, as we watch children how very individual their play becomes. A group of three girls, for instance, are playing with dolls. Vivienne is the mother. Her dolly is cuddled and fed, bathed and nursed before it is put in the cot. Gloria takes infinite care to arrange her doll in a pram which is later paraded for friends to admire. Beryl's doll lies naked on the floor while she designs and creates a fabulous wardrobe of clothes made from silks and velvets and fur.

Each child at the Infant School stage has come a long way in his play. There have been many developments since he played with his first toys and his own toes and limbs, finding out what belonged to him and what didn't, in an attempt to define his own identity.

Watching a child at play is a guide to his person. We notice the vital play of the healthy, interested child. We contrast it with the lethargic indifference of the same child when he is off-colour. We soon know when children play together which one is likely to become a leader and how each compares for intellect. We know how far developed they are socially. We are shown the child's deep-felt needs and receive guidance on how we can satisfy them.

Most of all we catch a reflection of the sheer joy of the child's delight in trivial things. Only a child can enjoy the insignificant. Eventually, we receive the message and know that the child plays because he must and that he will only develop fully if he plays fully. Knowing this we give full and unreserved recognition to the child's play as his means of development and adjustment, and we no longer feel guilty when we provide him with the time and facility to play. In this way we enable him to complete his purpose at this particular stage in development.

3

The integrated nature of learning

The new-born baby is a miracle of completeness. He is tiny and helpless, his crumpled face bearing little resemblance to what it will later become, yet the beginnings of all that the adult will be are already present. Those tiny ears, flattened against the face like scraps of paper, are fully equipped to perform their function. Each baby has a full complement of limbs and internal organs. All that is left for him to do is to grow and develop.

The baby has a great deal of developing to do. His development will be a total experience. He doesn't grow long legs and then longer arms: he grows as a whole. His growth is a harmonious process. What affects one aspect of his growth affects the whole organism. A child who is deaf, for instance, is not hampered only in hearing.[9] Unless he is given skilful help he will be slow to speak and to understand. He will have difficulty in communicating with others and will be slow to make friends. At a later stage his reading will be impaired and many sources of learning will be closed to him.

Each child is not only complete, he is individual. He will need to be studied and treated as a separate individual if he is to develop as he should.

At the beginning of the seventeenth century children were thought of as miniature adults. Portraits of children from this time show small-scale adults wearing miniature adult garments. Adults thought of children as material which they could mould and transform into useful citizens. It took educational reformers such as Comenius and Pestalozzi to point out that children should be recognised in their own right and that those responsible for the upbringing and education of children should focus their attention on the child himself, rather than the image they planned to mould him into.

Many adults still believe that school is a place where a child is instructed into becoming a useful citizen rather than into becoming himself. There are still many teachers who may sincerely believe that their work is child-centred and yet who, on closer examination of their motives, might find that they care more for the child being a credit to themselves than true to his own self. The joy and satisfaction to be found in teaching is a by-product of helping a child to discover what he is as a person and then assisting him to become that person and nobody else.

Fortunately the young baby has no speech and cannot learn from being told. He is thrown back upon his own resources and he learns at first-hand through his own efforts.[10] The child's sensory organs, his skin, his eyes, his ears and his sense of taste and smell, are his means of collecting information about the world around him. His first and most powerful means of communicating with his world is through his skin. Where his skin enters the openings into the body it is most sensitive, and the baby's mouth is where much learning starts. He will continue to refer things to his mouth for a very long time. (A more detailed study of sensory learning is made in *Discovering the Physical World* in this series.

Learning involves every aspect of the person. The young baby trying to communicate his needs to his mother uses all his resources. He waves his arms and legs about, he makes noises and expresses his emotions, he throws the whole of his person into his gestures. In school, the child struggling to put

The integrated nature of learning

his first intelligible symbols on paper uses as much physical effort as mental and when he has finished he needs the approval of his teacher and receives the satisfaction of achievement.

Each step the young child takes in his learning is closely related to the people around him. In retrospect we associate many of our most active moments in learning with some other person. A difficult task, for instance, was accomplished only when the right person helped.

Parents and teachers are equally the child's educators, and both need to co-operate so that the world of school and the world of home become one and the same. As teachers, we know the futility, for instance, of trying to help a child recognise words in a book when he is upset because his father has been 'locked away' and his mother has cried all night. We know that it isn't enough to sympathise, to put an arm round the child, and to stop pestering him with words. We need to understand his home background so that we know what his problem is, and then provide him with the kind of situation in school which will help him to come to terms with what troubles him. Later we shall examine in greater detail ways in which links between home and school can be forged.

Whitehead reminds us that 'you may not divide the seamless coat of learning'.[11] As adults we tend to separate differing areas of experience and give them names such as geography or history, art or mathematics. We are capable of handling abstract ideas and have a fairly clear concept of what we mean by these subject labels. The young child, however, doesn't understand these terms. He learns each thing as part of a whole situation and not as an isolated experience. He learns to discriminate, for example, between 'hot' and 'cold' or between 'boys' and 'girls' because he suffers the consequence of his choice. His first concern is to reduce the world to a pattern he can understand. He is readily interested in this and that, and we shall see how he learns many things related to his interests if they help him to understand.

Reaching out

Little children have very immature ideas about time. Their day flows on from one experience to another and the adult concept of a day fragmented into small parcels of time means little to them. The fact that a timetable allows them twenty minutes for reading and forty minutes for painting makes no sense at all.

They get absorbed in what they are doing and don't want to break off. One of the greatest joys in life is to be caught up in something which is more important than oneself. Children have the capacity for being caught up in the world of their imagination. Yet how often do we interrupt them 'because it is time to change to something else' and then complain that the child lacks concentration. We must consider ways whereby we can offer the child long unbroken stretches of time in which to become absorbed and to experience the satisfaction of concentrated effort.

Similar principles of wholeness apply to the structuring of the child's mind. His mind grows as his body grows, as part of his total system. The quality of his mind depends on his understanding and his understanding depends on the way in which his brain develops, on the condition of his sense organs, on the power of his limbs which enable him to reach out towards new experiences, on how he feels about the things he does and on the quality of provision made for his learning in the environment. Well motivated, the child exerts effort, and learning is active and intentional, until he gradually constructs for himself a map of his world which his mind can grasp.[12]

Learning starts at birth and continues throughout life. At about the age of five, the child is ready to extend his environment beyond the boundary of his home and immediate neighbourhood.[13] He enters school to continue his learning and certainly not to begin it. His experiences in school are for him a stage in the whole process. He will learn a lot in school, but his period of most active learning has already

The integrated nature of learning

taken place in the home and he will continue to learn in his home during his school years.

In school the child needs to see how the various aspects of his learning fit together and become part of his total development. He will see measurement used as a tool in physical education. He will find, in colour and form, that science becomes an intrinsic aspect of art. He will observe his own part of the earth and learn that historical understanding helps him to interpret what he sees. He will become aware that man's use of words links all learning and that the study of his own language is inherent in all that he does. Later he will come to understand the ordering of the universe and know that his study of life is also his education in belief.

Children learn from real things and from the things they do. Understanding comes through personal experience and not through being told. The teacher can put into words ideas discovered by the child, but if she tries to *tell* him what to think, he merely *repeats* what she says. Knowing grows within, from internalised experience.[14] There is all the difference in the world between personal knowledge and information acquired from others. Kahlil Gibran, the philosopher and poet from the Lebanon, has this to say about teaching in his book *The Prophet*:

'No man can reveal to you aught but that which already lies half-asleep in the dawning of your knowledge . . .

'If he [the teacher] is indeed wise he does not bid you enter the house of his wisdom, but rather leads you to the threshold of your own mind . . .

'For the vision of one man lends not its wings to another man.'

4

The pattern of learning

A group of five-year-old children present the teacher with a very wide range of behaviour. Peter can tie his own shoe-laces, while Roy can't manage his trouser buttons. Vickie holds back her sobs as Mother departs, but Susan makes no attempt to control her emotions. Mary can write her own name and has already filled a book with lively and colourful pictures, while John shows no interest at all in books and fills his scrap-book with formless slabs of paper.

Stephen is thin, with spectacles and a running nose. He shows little interest and his attention wanders in spite of an absorbing story. He is unable to respond to simple instructions and other children take little notice of him. Robert is well-built and vital, with bright eyes and an eager expression. His avid interest is readily stimulated. He asks many questions and listens when his questions are answered. Robert makes friends easily and already shows signs of becoming a leader. Robert apparently has all the gifts, while Stephen's gifts are meagre.

Each of these children has a different capacity for learning and each of them has reached a different stage in development. They all have much further to go and some will go further than others.

Parents and teachers who handle young children have always known that stage follows stage in development.

The pattern of learning

Mothers, describing their children, will say that 'Susan was more forward than John at that age. She said her first word at six months, but John here, at fifteen months, isn't through the babbling stage.' Mothers know that their children will sit and crawl before they stand and walk, and that they will learn to talk before they can learn to read. Ideas about maturation are not new to them, but in recent years the work of people such as Dr Tanner and Gesell has shown us how incomplete and formless our knowledge has been.[15] They have helped us to realise the extreme importance of growth and maturity when considering the education of the child.

The development of the child, both physical and mental, depends on how the child is endowed and on the unfolding of his qualities. It depends also on the opportunities for learning offered to the child by his environment. However strong the baby's legs and back may be, he would never learn to walk if he hadn't a floor to walk on, and what he ultimately achieves in the way of locomotion depends on the kind of challenge the walking area offers him.

Gesell provides us with a blueprint of a growth pattern. Each individual is born with this pattern predetermined. How far he can go is determined by his potential. We can forecast, for instance, how tall a person will become. At eighteen years he will be roughly twice as tall as he was at two. Forecasting of this kind is sometimes a guide to a child's career. Height is important, for instance, to the would-be policeman or ballet-dancer.

Although developmental limits are set by the pattern we inherit, few people reach their limit. Much depends on the emotional environment provided, and the happy, well-motivated person will achieve far more than the person who finds life a burden.

The pattern of development from birth to maturity and the sequence of stages through which the individual develops are the same for all people. But each individual is unique in the way his pattern varies from the norm. The rate at which he goes through the stages also varies.

Chronological age does not necessarily indicate the stage a child has reached in his growth pattern and we should think of the child's development in terms of stages rather than ages. The fact that a child has only reached a certain stage at any given age does not necessarily mean that he is a slow learner. He may be taking his time and may go further than the child whose abilities ripen quickly. His development may be erratic and a slow start may precede rapid development at later stages. Little research has been done on late development and many intelligent children become misfits because they are not understood.[16]

Growth is a continuous process – even during sleep – and each stage affects those which follow it. If we try to hurry a child through a stage, or by-pass a stage in education, the ultimate achievement is diminished. Full development is only possible when the child has lived each stage fully.

From time to time people become obsessed with the idea that if they force the pace or make a premature start, then the child will achieve more. They are usually disappointed. It is a law of nature that anything worth while takes time to grow and a premature start may create emotional blockage or result in superficial learning. Adequate opportunity at the right moment ensures maximum development.

How far do we recognise these facts when we devise a school system with the compulsory education of young children in mind? The State system is based on a pattern which evolved from what we once knew about the sequence of stages through which the child grows. Unfortunately the pattern was devised for that average child who occupies a mythical position midway between the widely varying patterns of real children.[17] We ignore the unique individuality of each child's variant from this norm, even though we may be well aware of it. Once the average pattern has been established and provided for it becomes administratively convenient to make all children fit the system, and only in recent years have any attempts been made to tailor the system to the individual child.[18]

There is perhaps more opportunity today for experimentation within the pattern of the State system, yet the State still legislates for the child according to his chronological age. When a child has had 1826 days' experience of the world he is ready to come into school. There he takes his place on the conveyor belt for about eleven years, after which most children are plucked off again and considered to be ready for adult life.

The Plowden Report[19] stated the case for a more flexible system, pointing out that children are born every day in the year and that entry to school should be staggered and the date decided by parents and teachers in consultation. More flexible arrangements for transfer between stages of education were also recommended; but none of these really faces the fact that it is the developmental age of the child which should determine the stage of his education.

In practice, within the existing system there is more room for flexibility than parents and teachers in general recognise. The head teachers of some Infant Schools, for instance, plan with parents to ease young children into the system by allowing for part-time attendance before registering them as full-time pupils. Opportunities for children to work at their own rate within the system are dealt with in a later chapter.

An important aspect of maturation is the occurrence of critical periods in growth. Abilities built into the child's pattern unfold at the appropriate stage, when his faculties provide him with the means of developing them. Given the right stimulus in the environment, the child responds and his ability develops. Effective learning depends on the teacher's skill in timing. Help offered too soon is wasted and can even build up a negative emotional response which can hinder learning. Help withheld for too long can mean that the most active period of learning a skill is by-passed and learning that skill may become difficult and sometimes impossible. How many of us adults feel that we had it in us to become poets or authors or politicians if our love of words had only been fostered at the right time?

Pamela's mother complained to her teacher: 'Pamela's been in school for nearly a term now and she hasn't been given a reader. Why aren't you teaching her to read?' The teacher glanced at the attractive library corner and explained: 'Pamela isn't ready yet'. To which Mother replied: 'If you haven't given her a reader how do you know she isn't ready?'

With forty children and their infinite variety of demands, how does the teacher recognise the moment when help with a skill will be most effective? Word recognition, which is what the parent meant by 'reading', like many other skills, is easier for the child at certain stages in learning.[20] The child himself gives the teacher the clues that indicate his readiness to learn. He shows interest and may even ask to be taught. 'What does this say?' is an indication of a developing skill. Some interests are merely experimental and temporary, but if the interest is sustained we can go ahead and help. After that, the rate of progress made by the child through practice will be a measure of his aptitude.

The teacher who listens to what the child says, who encourages him to talk, to ask questions and to think aloud, has the most accurate guide to the child's mind and ripening abilities she could possibly have. The adult who will listen is one of the child's best educators.

We have stressed the importance of the environment and of the part played by the interest shown by the child. John Dewey reminds us that 'an end which is the child's own carries him on to possess the means of its accomplishment'. We know that the child is an active participant in his own learning and that intentional learning is far more effective than incidental learning. We fail if we thrust the practice of a skill on the child before his aptitude for the skill has emerged, but we can make sure that the means of learning are available as soon as he is ready and we can stimulate the aptitude to emerge at the earliest possible moment and so give it the full span of growth available. If a child grows up in an unbookish environment, he has no chance to know whether he is interested in books or not.

No one has yet determined the precise contribution environmental and innate factors make to the child's learning. People with experience of young children feel the need for a harmonious relationship between these factors. They know that the child develops within the world of himself, they know that he develops an understanding of the environment without, and the more varied and interesting that environment is the more he reaches out to it. They know that the child's learning is his development as a person and that this development is the result of interaction between the world within the child and the world which surrounds him. Learning is the bridge between the two.

We cannot teach aptitudes, but we can encourage them to emerge and then provide the opportunities for them to be used with purpose. The child is born with the ability to learn, but we are responsible for the full development of his abilities.

Sometimes we recognise these principles, sometimes to the detriment of the child's learning we try to ignore them. We are prepared to wait until the child's teeth erupt before we expect him to chew, to wait until his muscles develop before we expect him to walk; we don't try to make him use artificial teeth or crutches to anticipate the process. Yet adults are often guilty of trying to drill children into the mechanical manipulation of numbers before their ideas of these numbers develop, and into vocalising printed words before experience has given these words meaning. Then we wonder why the child makes such slow progress. If learning is to be fully effective, we need to watch for the moment of readiness to learn, and begin then. We must remember, too, that if we miss the best moment, learning becomes difficult, and sometimes impossible.

5

The individuality of the child

The child's individuality contributes more to the fascination of teaching than any other factor. His unique qualities are most readily observed during his first year in school, before school education has attempted to iron out many of his differences and persuaded his unique nature to conform to the cultural pattern.

We do not expect the child of five to conform very closely to the pattern prescribed by society. Consequently he does not hesitate to show us what he is and how he feels about people and things. In the spontaneous behaviour of children we can observe the reality of childhood in all its variety. It is the child's spontaneity which endears him to us and yet we try so soon to take it away from him and encourage him to be a 'good' boy, i.e. to submit to our wishes.

For the first week or two in school a child may appear to make little response to this dramatic change in his environment. Once he feels well established and freed from the restrictions of his home, his individual characteristics become emphasised, until even his own mother 'can't believe that's our Johnny'.

If we stand a group of five-year-old children in a row we are struck by the range of physical appearances. Heights can vary by anything up to twelve inches. Anne is slight with small bones. She appears almost insubstantial, while Lorna is 'bonny' and promises to become an Amazon. There is a firm link between the mind and the body. We know by their expression and the way in which children move and play that Robert is likely to become a high-flyer, whereas William may achieve little however hard he struggles.

As we get to know these children better we recognise their different natures and attitudes and glimpse something of the way they will deal with life. Terry bursts upon you, his warm nature flows out and evokes a warm response in his direction. Robin hangs on to his cap and hugs a small packet of biscuits against his chest, as though he fears you would prise them away from him.

The head teacher holding a school service faces 240 children. In her time she has watched over the early development of perhaps two or three thousand children. Not once has she seen a pattern repeated. Individuality is the perpetual phenomenon of human nature. Try as we will, we cannot avoid taking it into account when we plan the education of young children.

There are many ways in which children differ. Their bodies differ in size, mobility and strength. No amount of physical training will make the short boy become a tall one. Intelligence varies: not only in degree, but also in kind. Intelligence is not a given power one can measure. Teachers tend to possess academic intellect and the educational system emphasises the importance of academic qualities. Not enough recognition is given to the child who is creatively intelligent, or socially intelligent, and the force of tradition is such that practical intelligence tends to be given a lower rating.

Children vary emotionally, and the emotional environment of the child's early years determines whether he will respond joyfully to life or withdraw from it.[21] Much the same differences exist between children socially. We do not expect every child to make friends easily, or even to find more satisfaction in the company of others than he does when left to his own devices.

Reaching out

In the spontaneous behaviour of the child at five we see foreshadowed the person he will become deep down, even though he may from time to time acquire a veneer which simulates other patterns.

These vast differences are due partly to inheritance and partly to the environment within which the child develops. At the moment of conception the individual is endowed with certain characteristics. From each parent he receives 23 chromosomes and each chromosome carries strings of genes, which in turn transmit characteristics from parent to child. The assortment of genes inherited by the child is a matter of chance, and as there is no way of controlling the assortment, each child's combination of characteristics is different from everyone else's.[22]

Each individual has the same range of traits in his personality, but the quality of each trait varies in character with the individual. Each child has a streak of generosity in his nature, but where Judy finds pleasure in sharing her sweets with a friend, Rita will offer one grudgingly because it is the thing to do, and Sue will hide hers in the doll's pram.

The environment within which these traits unfold has a profound effect on the outcome. Even children in the same home are brought up in different worlds. They are born at different times, hold different positions in the family, stimulate different responses from people and eventually make different friends and do different things.[23]

Some parents fondly believe that because 'John is the spitting image of his father' he has inherited all of his father's characteristics. They fail to take into account the powerful influence of parental attitudes and the fact that a child tends to adopt the image his parents provide as the pattern of what he should become. Had John been adopted and brought up in a different family he would have considerably less resemblance to his father.

Many teachers and parents find it difficult to accept the

The individuality of the child

child's individuality. We are very powerful influences in the child's life, and it is tempting to try to mould the child into what we would like him to be and sometimes into a pale image of what we ourselves would like to have been. We know that children differ in physical build, in rates of growth, and in their abilities. As adults they will differ very much from one another. We don't expect all children of the same age to take the same size of clothes. Yet sometimes we try in school to teach a whole group of children the same thing at the same time and age. We even try to impose on them adult patterns of perfection.

There are some Infant Schools, for example, where patient hours are spent in training children to perfect those balls and sticks which form print. Identical pages of print are displayed on the wall. Unless they bear the child's name not even their owners can identify them. The whole aim is to eradicate individuality in style, when handwriting, as an intimate art form, should express the individual's personality.

When the child thwarts us we sometimes resent his individuality. We try to tell him what to think when he has thoughts of his own. We try to put our mind between the child and his experience. We give him a rich array of paints, perhaps, and then hover over him while he expresses the idea in our mind on his paper. We may even tell him what to paint, to make a picture of this or that, when the paint is stirring his own mind into vivid images.

The child can't be what he isn't. It is our job to accept him as different from ourselves, instead of using him as a means of expressing and confirming our own individuality. We must avoid asserting our own individuality at his expense and we need to give him credit for knowing better than we do where his interests lie.

A student on teaching practice assembled a wonderful collection of fossils. She arranged them carefully and selected appropriate reference books, in which the children could

Reaching out

follow up their initial interest. One little girl returned again and again to the display. She held one of the fossils and fingered it pensively. The student indicated an attractive reference book.

'Would you like to find out more about the fossil?' she suggested.

The little girl shook her head. 'No, thank you,' she murmured and walked away, leaving the fossil as though she had lost interest.

In spite of her disappointment the student left the child alone. An hour later she found her in the painting corner. She was putting the finishing strokes to a swirling riot of colour, obviously inspired by the fossil shape. This was the child's way of understanding the fossil which interested her. What the fossil could tell her itself was more important at this stage than information found in a reference book.

People who visit schools regularly become sensitive to the atmosphere created by the people who work in them. The sincerity of the school which puts the real interests of children first permeates all that goes on in the school, and one cannot fail to recognise and respect it.

At all stages a person's name is highly important to him. We respond immediately whenever we hear our own name. Nothing pleases us more than to know that our name is remembered. One of the first words a child likes to write is his own name, and the sight of his name on a peg in the cloakroom gives him a sense of security and the knowledge that he belongs. A person's name represents his unique individuality.

We firmly believe that each one of us is important and religious belief is founded on the fact that the individual matters because of what he is as an individual. Even the child of Infant School age wonders at the fact that no one else is quite like himself and that his mother and teacher can recognise him amongst all the others.

The individuality of the child

The very fact that the pattern is never repeated is in itself sufficient to confirm the miracle of creation. A man is known even by his finger-prints. The clothes he wears and the tools he uses bear the mark of his individuality. The artist depends on his unique mode of interpretation and this is what makes each man of interest to others. In the words of Goethe, 'Nature seems to have staked everything on individuality'.

It is not surprising that Man sees himself as being in the image of God. How otherwise can he ultimately account for his own difference unless he sees within himself a unique spark given him directly by the Creator? Science accounts for so much, but does not in itself offer the complete explanation for something which is as important to man as life itself.

A person only knows he lives when he knows he counts as someone special. He requires first and foremost to be needed and respected. There are so many of us that unless we can feel that we matter as separate persons then the life we have is meaningless.

The child is in an even more difficult position. His smallness and his helplessness make him feel insignificant. Only his uniqueness can attract the attention which guarantees him recognition. He would rather be ill-treated than disregarded.

But we must go further than this to help the child. Not only must he feel he belongs and counts and knows he is accepted, he must also know that we approve of him. How else can he be encouraged to become what he is intended to be? And how can he do this if we set ourselves up as a pattern or prescribe other patterns and try to make him become them? Above all else we must help the child to discover his own individual pattern and to like it when he finds it, and then we must help him to nourish his individuality towards its ultimate maturity.

6

The developing person

We are educating our children to take their place in a complex society, where personality plays the leading role in successful adjustment. In our cultural group personality is highly prized and is often the determining factor in appointment to a job. Paper qualifications take us so far and then a personal interview decides the issue. Consequently teachers and parents regard the development of sound personality patterns as extremely important. In fact, the aim of education today could be defined as the fullest possible development of the child's personality. This is what we mean by *child-centred* education, or education which is centred in the nature of the child.

Learning plays a very important role in the development of personality. Indeed, personality represents all a man has learned as an individual, and living, development, learning and personality are basically aspects of a single process. They are the outcome of the individual's attempts to survive.

As educators of the young it is important for us to understand the nature of personality and the way in which it develops. We are then in a good position to help the child accomplish his task successfully. From the wealth of clinical information available we will try to select those factors which significantly affect parents and teachers.

The developing person

Personality consists of both what a person is and the way in which he appears to others. The important components of the personality pattern are the basic 'core' (the idea the person has of himself) and the traits which develop in keeping with the nature of that 'core'. The idea the child has of himself will have a powerful influence on the ultimate pattern of his personality, and those who are responsible for the child in his early years are inextricably bound up in his own idea of self. We must accordingly know what this responsibility is.

Mrs Nameless came into school dragging a very reluctant Ernest. Thirty-six busy children stopped what they were doing as the classroom door burst open and Ernest was precipitated into the room with Mother's foot behind him.

'Here!' she shrieked. 'He's all yours. See what you can do. He's useless and I'm fed up with the sight of his sniffling nose. He's been pinching eggs from the allotments again instead of coming to school and I can't do nowt wi' 'im.'

What does Ernest start with? What idea has he got of himself? His mother makes it obvious that she hasn't much of an opinion of him and she doesn't seem disposed to help him make himself any more acceptable.

Ernest's idea of himself is rooted in the temperament, intellect and physique he was born with. As he becomes aware of himself he finds that he is thin and undersized, with a perpetual running nose which is due to sinus trouble and which his mother hasn't bothered to remedy. He isn't dull enough to remain in blissful ignorance of the fact that others are better off than himself. Temperamentally he has a sense of adventure and finds little to satisfy it at home. He grows up in an atmosphere of conflict and confusion, where anything worth while is too much trouble, and where you keep what you find and you're in luck if you can get away with it. He sees himself as a poor thing and is prepared to take it out of those who are better endowed.

Reaching out

A child catches his ideas of himself from the image of himself which others hold up to him. What people say to him and about him and the way they treat him show him what he is. It is from his parents and family that a child gets his first idea about what he is like and what he is likely to become. The child brings this primary idea of himself into school; it influences the idea given him within the wider circle of people outside his family. Mark, for instance, has obviously been the centre of affection. His self-idea differs fundamentally from the idea Ernest holds of himself. Mark is a charming and gifted child. He expects people to indulge him and is generous in return. He has so much, he can afford to lavish affection on others. When people neglect him he is puzzled. Because he is intelligent, sensitive and hasn't been spoilt, he will learn how to earn the approval of others rather than come to expect it.

Peter is intelligent, lissom and very anxious to please. His interest is easily attracted and held. Once he has set himself a job to do, he pursues his purpose with an intensity which leaves him exhausted. His parents are ambitious for Peter and have set him levels of attainment which may overstretch him. School will need to help Peter enjoy his work and make him concentrate less on striving after the approval of an adult.

The importance of personal relationships cannot be overemphasised. We have seen how people represent the child's most challenging learning situation. All the people he meets in school are in some way responsible for shaping his developing personality, but the people he loves and admires influence him most of all.

The foundation of the child's personal pattern has been laid in the home, but in school he will find many opportunities for learning that his home has not been able to provide. What he becomes as a person is the result of what he learns. In his pre-school years he learned much from his parents and

The developing person

he will continue to learn from them, although for a time the new learning situations in school may appear to be more influential.

The first thing that school offers him is the companionship of other children. He may at times learn more from being with them than he does from his teacher. He will need to adjust to them emotionally and socially, he will extend himself physically to prove himself to them, and his mind will respond to the challenge he meets in the minds of other children.

The young child at this stage is still dependent on the adult to a certain extent and his teacher will become a significant person in his life. She is a different person from his mother, and because she is different she can spark off aspects of his personality that would have remained dormant within the life of the home. 'Personality is like a harp with many strings. Not all the strings are plucked at once and some may lie silent throughout life.' (From *The Integrity of Personality* by Anthony Storr.)

The child will strive to earn his teacher's approval. If he likes her he will throw all his resources into pleasing her. What she approves of in him will become more definitely established. Her own personality will become a pattern he emulates. To a certain extent he will try to model his developing self on her. A group of children reflect the personality of their teacher in quite a terrifying way.

There are other people in school besides children and teachers. There is the caretaker who is handy with tools and does interesting things in the boiler-house. Some children in the Infant School think that because he is the only man in the school, he is the head of it. All the children in the school know him and his influence is powerful.

There are the motherly people who help at lunchtime, there is the plumber who mends burst pipes, the lady who cooks dinner for hungry children, the lady who takes care of dinner tickets. Sometimes there are important visitors who

Reaching out

look at children's work and ask questions, and men who bring the milk or coke or come with interesting instruments to measure the building.

Watching children in their spontaneous play, we realise how quick they are to absorb parts of the personalities of those who interest them. Janet in her lace curtains *is* the important visitor to the school who admired Janet's picture on the wall. Ron, spitting skilfully into the playground wastebin, *is* the bricklayer who helped to build the cloakroom extension.

All these people are part of the widening group of relationships the child makes once he comes into school. All he learns from them is fitted into the emerging pattern of his person. They are helping him to reach out towards the adult he will become.

We recognise the importance of these factors, and in school we provide particular opportunities for the child to discover the pattern of his personality and to develop it as his unique gift.

Entry to school gives a child his first opportunity to get to know himself as a person apart from his family. Contrary to what many mothers believe, most children enjoy this step towards independence.

Mother brought Dave into school. She explained that he was shy and, as the school was vertically grouped, asked if he could go in with his sister Georgina until he got used to being away from home. The headmistress agreed. A few days later Dave approached her.

'I want to go in another class', he said. 'I don't want our Georgina. I see her at home.'

When the child becomes one of a group of children outside his family circle, they soon show him what they think about him, and so help him to get a more objective view of himself than he could have gained at home. In school the child finds a range of new materials with which to express what he feels and reflect the content of his mind. The impression he leaves on clay, on paper, in the models he constructs, and the way he handles these things show him something of himself. In dramatic play he can experiment with being a number of selves. In handling equipment or struggling to master new skills he finds out what kind of person he is and how he fits into the pattern of his group.

By offering him choice from a wide range of interests, the teacher enables him to select the job suited to him. She encourages him in his efforts, shares his interests, lends her enthusiasm to reinforce his effort, and so, between them, teacher and child nourish the child's unique qualities, enabling him to become truly himself and to rejoice in it.

Richard was quiet and withdrawn. He had intelligent parents and a gifted brother Robert, two years older than himself. The parents tried hard to treat their children as equals, but their warm approval of Robert's attainments overshadowed Richard. He felt inadequate and did not understand that being younger in itself meant that he couldn't do what Robert could do.

The fact that Richard loved and admired his parents and brother intensely made matters worse. It widened the gap between what he was and what he wanted to be in order to compare favourably with Robert. Richard invented an imaginary companion as a form of compensation and 'Nicki' was introduced into every picture Richard drew. Richard was clearly superior to 'Nicki' – at least he had control over him.

Richard's teacher was interested in music and a well-organised sound-making corner occupied a permanent place in her classroom. This became Richard's favourite retreat. Here he displayed a sensitive and creative approach towards sounds and was soon making his own tunes on the chime-bars. His teacher showed him how to write them down. When Richard took home his first 'composition' and fingered it out on the piano, the delight of his parents was completely spontaneous. Richard knew the difference between what they felt about this achievement and what they had felt about things he struggled to do. His confidence had taken roots and slowly developed; he forgot about 'Nicki' and delighted in being himself.

Our children are growing up in a society where personality is important, because it determines the recognition afforded to the individual in his group. If child-centred education means anything, it stands for a way of life for the child which will enable him to develop fully as the person he is.

7

The importance of environment

Sharon and two of her friends arrived at school one morning carrying a jam jar. The toad at the bottom of the jar had been found in Sharon's garden. Ten minutes later Sharon's teacher rescued the toad from being committed to the aquarium. 'Toads don't live *in* water,' she explained. 'We'll fetch the book on frogs, toads and newts from the library and find out how he does live. You didn't find the toad in the water, did you?'

Later on in the morning the toad was taken into the school service as a treasure to share with the whole school. When the local inspector arrived to see the headmistress the toad was brought in to show 'Sir' too.

'She can jump,' the children informed 'Sir'. 'She can jump high.'

The toad was placed on the carpet and a pencil extended in front of her. Sharon tickled the back of the toad's neck and she obliged. 'Sir' rose to the occasion.

'How high does she jump?' he enquired.

The children fetched a ruler and decided that the toad's jump was nine inches, which was 'very high for anybody so little'. Sharon lifted Toad back into the jam jar.

'She doesn't weigh very much,' she said thoughtfully. With a fresh idea in mind, the children went back to their classroom.

Reaching out

At lunchtime the teacher decided 'it's rather hot in here for Toad. I think she'd be happier back in Sharon's garden.' Rather reluctantly the children agreed. 'But they haven't all seen what she can do,' they complained.

'You could write it all in a book,' the teacher suggested. 'If we put the book in the library corner everyone who comes to the school can read about Toad.'

In the afternoon Sharon and her two friends wrote their book. This was the first book Sharon had made and she needed her teacher's help with the words. 'If we're writing a book about Toad,' she said, 'we must give her a name.' The book was illustrated and contained the following observations.

'This is Prudens our toad . . . This is Prudens in the tank . . . We found it in Sharon's garden . . . Toads lay eggs in a pond. The eggs hatch into tadpoles . . . Toads do not live in water . . . She can jump nine inches . . . She weighs an ounce.'

Sharon and her friends were six years old. Between them during the day they had taken up perhaps fifteen minutes of their teacher's time. They had used a number of other people and books to extend their discovery of toads. They worked in a classroom of forty children whose ages ranged from five to seven. What were some of the other thirty-seven children doing that day?

At one large table children were making pictures from odds and ends of all kinds. José's picture was a doll with a round cheese-box face. She had given her a skirt cut from a piece of green velvet. She sat stroking the soft fabric scraps still left in her hand and said, 'She must have a cardigan.'

She spread out the scraps and started to plan how the complicated shapes could be cut from her meagre remnants. Her mathematical ingenuity enabled her to provide the required cardigan.

At the same table an older boy struggled with an old sieve and some pieces of strong wire. 'It's Jodrell Bank,' he explained. 'I saw it when I went with my Dad on Sunday and he says

The importance of environment

it's 250 feet across. It's enormous.' The colander bowl in his hand at that moment was the wonderful telescope itself. At this point his creative effort was his way of finding out about the telescope. His teacher made sure that a good reference book was available in the library corner, but didn't interrupt the child's imaginative thinking at that stage.

Five-year-old Keith at the water trolley was absorbed in pouring from one vessel to another. His attention eventually concentrated on the water in the polythene jug. He lifted it against the light and tipped it this way and that, keeping a vigilant eye on the level of the water. He noticed his teacher and delight flushed his face as he explained: 'It stays the same. It always stays the same.' He had discovered one of the basic principles of the behaviour of water and from now on the knowledge would be his.

In another school children of the same age-range appeared at first glance to be working in much the same way. The classroom was lively with plenty of interesting materials. Children were working individually and in small groups. Closer observation revealed significant differences between the two schools.

Five-year-old Ian sat in front of a large outline picture of a giraffe. He was cutting small pieces with great care from a piece of yellow and brown material. He pasted each piece as he cut it into the shape on the paper. He covered one foot and continued up the leg, glancing from time to time at the vast expanse to be filled. When asked about his picture he explained, 'We're making a frieze about animals and Miss C said I had to make the giraffe.' He pointed to the wide band of paper which ran the length of the wall. 'The giraffe will go at the end.'

Ten minutes later Ian's patience was running out. His pieces were now the size of a florin and the giraffe was practically filled in. Six of Ian's friends were likewise engaged in making animal pictures for the teacher's frieze. Lacking Ian's initiative, they were clearly prepared to carry on for the rest of the afternoon. A number of other children were twisting scraps of green tissue paper to paste on to the frieze to represent undergrowth.

In other parts of the room a number of activities occupied the rest of the class. Three children at the sand table were experimenting with a small heap of dry sand, but their equipment, a bucket and a sieve, didn't take them very far. At the weighing table four children were following instructions on printed cards and recording their findings. Two children were playing number lotto.

At another table four children were making books about birds. Their little books were nicely illustrated and full of information. Both pictures and information were identical with the reference books open in front of them.

The situation in both schools was far removed from formal class teaching. Opportunities were varied and the provision of materials had received attention. The children were active in their learning, but the quality of this varied considerably.

In the first school learning stemmed from the children's own interests. Sharon brought her source of interest into school and found means of extending it. Several kinds of learning – reading, writing, measuring and natural history – sprang from the same interest. Material in the school sparked off interest in other children. Stimulating material was provided and the teacher's knowledge of its educative value guided her choice in what she put before the child. The child, exploring it, decided what he would do with it. He was in every sense of the term an active agent in his own learning. The teacher let the material speak to the child, stimulating him according to what he was able and ready to learn. The child's own purpose led him in a number of different directions, and José, for instance, intent on creating a picture, became unwittingly involved in a mathematical experience.

In the second school the teacher had decided in advance

The importance of environment

what the child should learn from material she provided. The frieze originated in her mind and she used the children to give practical expression to her idea. She even gave Ian material of the right colour. Most of the other children in the room were obeying instructions on cards, or reproducing the work of others. Even the freedom to explore the properties of sand was restricted by the limits to the equipment available.

Sometimes teachers believe that, because the child is working individually, such learning is informal. But this kind of learning can be every bit as formal and directed as the learning in a formal class lesson. Opportunities for spontaneous learning stem from the educational aims of the teacher. The mere provision of material, equipment and individual work does not in itself constitute an informal approach.

There is a world of difference between instruction and self-activated learning, between directed activity and spontaneous investigation. These differences are reflected in the vitality of the educational opportunity offered the child. The fundamental difference between an education centred in the child's needs and one based on formal tuition or training is the difference between helping the child to understand and telling him what to do and think.

Within the spontaneous learning situation the interest of the whole class can be stimulated around a single topic. The teacher who introduces a vivid green lizard into her classroom is sure to catch the attention of every child. The need for a class lesson occurs quite naturally from time to time, because sometimes the interests of every child in a group coincide. Child-centred education is not so much a particular set of methods or techniques as an attitude towards children. A deep understanding of the way in which children learn is the basic equipment of the teacher. The methods she uses will stem from this.

A good environment offers material which will spark off interests in the minds of children with very varying abilities and inclinations. It will enable each child to further his own interests and will then challenge him further. It demands his utmost effort and then shows him further vistas of interest, keeping him perpetually reaching out. It includes a degree of frustration or tension without which effort tends to wane.

The environment should be well, but not over, endowed. Some schools, in their anxiety to provide variety, become museums. Every conceivable form of stimulation clutters the child's surroundings. There is nowhere for the eye to rest, no corner for meditation and no breathing space during which the child can consolidate. Perpetual stimulation allows no time for inner growth. The fallow periods are essential if the child is to possess harmony in his spirit and that inner peace which sustains him. The opportunity to reflect is essential to the development of sound thinking.

In the end the mind of the teacher is the most powerful influence in any classroom. What she knows and believes about children will create the atmosphere affecting their learning. What she does in every single situation originates in what she thinks. The provision of the right environment starts in her mind. What the child makes of the environment provides evidence of her interest and enthusiasm. The quality of his learning depends on where she puts the emphasis. If her ultimate aim for the child is to produce results which bring her recognition and satisfaction, the emphasis is on the end-product rather than on the process. If her ultimate aim is for the full development of the child as a person, the emphasis is on the process, which may or may not produce overt expressions of success other than the child's ability to live successfully. There is a vast difference between the two aims, and we must be clear before we start what our plans for the child really are.

8

Preparing the environment

Learning starts at birth and is very rapid during the early years. The five-year-old enters school to carry on with his learning. The teacher takes him up at the stage of development he has reached and carries him on from there. The child needs to find in school much that is familiar, together with new and more challenging experiences which will extend the work done in the home.

The provision the teacher makes in the classroom is her scheme of work, and the experiences she offers the child determine the direction of his learning. She guides his attention towards worth-while opportunities, but what he learns from them depends on his individual interest and ability.

Children vary very widely in their needs and the teacher must consequently provide a wide range of experiences. We do not expect every child to explore all the situations, since each is unique in his needs and will select from his environment the job which has meaning for him. Andrew, for example, coming from a 'professional' home where books are prized above tools and a bench, may need to spend quite a lot of time hammering nails into wood. Later he will take up his books as well.

The materials and situations from which the teacher makes her selection are not limited to those found in school. The market, shops and traffic along the road, trees and living things which inhabit the park, the sun and the atmosphere with its exciting weather phenomena, are all available as sources of learning. Most important of all to the child are people. Children learn as much from one another as they do from the teacher. Every adult the child meets in the person of caretaker, policeman, school doctor or lunchtime supervisor is, in some way, his educator. The teacher provides the opportunity for him to make his contacts and also helps him to get the best out of them.

Equipping the child's environment is not enough, however. Unless the teacher is fully aware of the learning possibilities of environmental situations, very few children will get maximum benefit from what they do. The teacher, as we have seen, does not decide what the child *will* discover but, if she knows what he *can* discover, by asking the right question or by introducing a further challenge at the right moment she will lead him almost unconsciously towards what can be found.

The Wendy House, for instance, is sometimes taken for granted. Many teachers provide and maintain attractive equipment for domestic play, without really considering what the child can gain from using it.

In the Wendy House the child is going to play out many real-life situations: emotional and social problems will find expression here. For instance, a child can release a good deal of angry resentment by taking it out on a doll. Dramatic and imaginative play will help him also to grow in mind and spirit. Simple equipment which leaves much to the child's imagination offers him more scope than the elaborate tea-sets and cooking stoves which catch the eye of the adult. The intellectual content of domestic play will be considered more fully in other parts of this work.

Bricks challenge the imagination. When playing with bricks, a child is introduced to the principles of design and construction. He will learn how to build a wall that is strong and why the right angle is economical. He will add to his

Preparing the environment

vocabulary words describing shape, size and quantity. Bricks that are big enough to enable him to build 'real' edifices provide more learning opportunity than bricks the size of a matchbox. The most popular bricks in one school were a collection left by the contractor on a construction job. They cost nothing.

Water and sand are man's natural materials. By exploring their properties and observing their behaviour a child is introduced to a great many scientific principles. Such materials provide, too, emotional and creative outlets. They should be so situated that the teacher can keep a close watch on what is happening. The introduction of simple equipment such as transparent tubing, which allows a child to see what is happening between water and air, tins with holes at varying levels to demonstrate the effect of water pressure, squeeze bottles and containers of various shapes and sizes, will show a child how water behaves. An empty five-gallon polythene sherry container, which many wine stores will supply free, provides running water when there is no sink in the classroom.

Sand behaves differently when it is wet. Why does wet sand stick together and hold the shape of a sand pie? Why does dry sand assume the shape of a cone when poured? If we cut across a cone shaped from wet sand at different angles, what shapes do we find? In these simple ways we can stretch children in their exploration.

Apart from the emotional and creative outlet they provide, materials such as clay and wood are part of the child's discipline. They present him with problems and, in order to achieve the result he desires, he has to learn how they should be handled.

In the paint corner, provision for four children to paint at a time may be sufficient. Signing up on a rota is an incentive to master the writing of one's name. Here a child should find a variety of papers, such as sugar paper, unprinted newsreel and kitchen paper, in different shapes and sizes. A range of paints is also inspirational: wet and dry powder paint, paint mixed with paste, wall paint or, sometimes, oil paint together with sawdust, wood shavings, broken egg-shells, seeds and so on, to give texture, and a range of thick and thin paint brushes – all these enlarge a child's creative opportunity. Sacking is a very satisfying background for paint, as is newspaper coated with whitewash.

Pictures can be made from a wide variety of media other than paint, crayon or charcoal. Fabrics, shells, wheat, feathers, tin-foil and sequins pasted on to a background give pictures with 'body'. Sometimes ideas for pictures are stimulated by the materials provided; at other times the materials are used for carrying out ideas arising from a child's personal experience.

A well-equipped writing-table should inspire children to put down their thoughts on paper in the form of pictures and words. Plain and tinted paper free from the restriction of lines, pencils, crayons, scissors, a tray full of pictures to paste in books, and a stapling machine to fasten pages together will encourage children to explore their use of words. Sometimes the teacher can make a book to fit a child's particular requirements. A box of ready-made books, each containing only a few pages, should also be available in the writing corner.

A 'beanstalk', or tier of vegetable racks, will hold an assortment of waste materials. Tomato boxes, painted and nailed to upright supports, cost only a few pence. If castors are added, the whole construction becomes mobile.

Waste materials for creative work should be as interesting and challenging as possible, but a tattered collection of detergent packets and orange boxes will stimulate no child's imagination. Parents should be encouraged to supply material. This, too, is a way of enlisting the interest of parents, helping them to understand unfamiliar ways of learning. The father who brings in an old wireless set is interested in what happens to it. When he knows what the child has discovered about magnets and copper wire and the use he has made of them, modern ideas begin to make sense to him.

One of the chief characteristics of young children is their curiosity. It is through the satisfaction of this emotion that the child learns about the world around him. The child's curiosity and the need to explore are the teacher's most powerful aids. The range of interests should extend beyond the natural investigation of living things to the interesting and curious in every aspect of life. A piece of bark, the skeleton of a leaf, wool from a sheep's back, stones from the garden, odds and ends of electrical equipment . . . the range is unlimited. Rust from a nail is as interesting a starting-point as the tropical tree in Kew Gardens.

An essential process in learning is the need to identify with other people. A collection of simple dressing-up materials will help children to find out in some measure what it feels like to be a mother or a bus conductor, a policeman or a king. Dramatic play provides the opportunity to channel emotion, to play out frightening situations and to give expression to an active imagination. For their play, children do not need elaborate props. Old lace curtains will create a princess, a bride, or a fairy. A length of swirling black material, a scrap of fur, something that glitters, a fireman's helmet, a pair of high-heeled shoes *suggest*; imagination creates the rest. Children are more likely to keep these things tidy if they are stored simply, for instance by hanging them over a rail or a clothes-horse.

On a measuring and weighing table, real instruments are in themselves a source of mathematical exploration. A surveyor's tape, a Gunter's chain, callipers, a metronome, a barometer and a micrometer are fruitful starting-points. These are precision instruments which need to be treated with great respect; children will require the help of the teacher to find out about them. But how much more will the child learn from handling the Gunter's chain with its hundred links than from cheap kitchen scales which are forever out of balance? In learning, quality is more important than quantity, and children learn more from one piece of accurate equipment than they do from half a dozen inferior tools.

Reaching out

In schools which favour a continuous day, the drinking of milk is incidental. A milk corner, with attractive mats and flowers on the table, accommodates from four to five children. Within reason, children take milk when they wish and this corner becomes an essential part of their social training.

The background to learning is a good supply of books, arranged in such a way that they are easily accessible to the child when he needs them. They should be displayed at eye-level, with the covers showing. Sometimes appropriate books can be associated with displays and objects of interest. The way children use books in school is an index to the learning that is taking place there.

Insufficient attention is often paid to the outdoor environment. A good collection of junk in the form of old tyres, old packing-crates, a plank and a ladder, little cider barrels obtained from a brewery, a thick rope, the steering wheel from an old car, add interest to a concrete playground. There is a limitless variety of inexpensive material which can be transformed into objects which encourage imaginative construction. Play with the boxes is one of the most popular outlets, particularly for boys, who can here channel their aggressive energy into co-operative, constructive activity.

Many of our children find little in their homes to promote the growth of the spirit. In every school there should be some corner reserved for displays of unusual and beautiful objects and the lovely things made by children's hands. They will learn to love and respect things which are pleasant to see, feel and hear. Using such treasures to form a focal part of the school service fosters a child's protective respect for them. A piece of good pottery, a length of silk, a delicate piece of embroidery or a crystal jar can be left where children can enjoy them at their leisure.

Children cannot learn in a vacuum. In this brief survey we have tried to consider a selection of materials which inspire learning and also catch a glimpse here and there of the underlying purpose behind them.

9

Working together

The school community consists essentially of a large number of children in the care of a small number of adults. For administrative reasons it is convenient to group the children into class units, each in the charge of one teacher. The criteria by which we select these groups are in many ways related to the views we hold about education. Where the work is teacher-directed and the children are expected to achieve set standards in defined aspects of learning, grouping according to chronological age is felt to be an advantage. Where the class is taught as a single unit, grading the children according to academic ability reduces the range of performance in a single class. We find chronological grouping and sometimes streaming in many Infant Schools.

If the child is recognised as an individual and encouraged to work at his own pace and with the 'grain' of his personality, the idea of having children of similar age working together becomes pointless and artificial. The importance of organising the school to meet the needs of the child takes precedence, as far as possible, over administrative convenience. Many Infant Schools have adopted the idea of vertical grouping, so that we have children of mixed ages in each class unit.

A brief history of the development of this form of organisation in one school will illustrate some of the claims made in its favour.

Reaching out

The events described took place in 1954 in an Infant School of 500 children where the annual intake was in the region of 190, or the size of five class units. It was common practice at that time to promote children at the beginning of each term, in order to make room for new entrants. The teachers in this school were so worried about the unsettling effects of this procedure and the lack of emotional continuity that they decided to try an experiment. In the following September the school opened with five reception classes, each of which contained a small nucleus of six-year-old children. By the end of the year there was an age-range of eighteen months in these classes.

The children in these classes benefited by continuity and in a number of unexpected ways. In fact, there were so many exciting developments that the teachers suggested that the seven-year-old children should also share these benefits and in the following year the whole school was organised into twelve units, each of which covered the full age-range of the school.

The changes were made to meet the needs of the children and not because the headmistress wanted to try out a theory. Although this way of grouping children produced a few problems, the advantages easily outweighed them. Parents and teachers were unanimous in their decision to establish these arrangements and so were able to assess the long-term benefits to the child.

They found that on admission children join in small numbers an established group, and this provides a settled, secure atmosphere for the child leaving home for the first time. In school he finds an ordered pattern of life with companions who know their way around and can help him to find his niche. Also, as there are only four or five new children admitted to each class at a time, the teacher can give each of them a fair amount of attention.

Vertical grouping emphasises the individuality of children.

Working together

Class teaching would be quite impossible, as the children are as mixed as possible in every way. The provision made must be comprehensive, and this in itself ensures that the interests of each child are catered for at various stages.

With older and younger children working together, a family atmosphere is created. The younger child finds in the more developed child someone who understands his problems – often better than the teacher. He views with respect the skill of the seven-year-old and sees where his efforts can lead him. Older children benefit from the satisfaction of being able to help younger ones. The less able older child who is struggling with the early stages of reading is not conspicuous. Sometimes older children, in moments of stress, feel the need to revert to easy and familiar tasks, and with this system they can do so without losing face.

With this form of organisation there is no concentration of any one particular age-group. At no time is the teacher confronted with forty five-year-olds unable to tie their own shoe-laces, or forty six-year-olds needing extra help at a crucial stage in learning to read. Gang play never gets out of hand, because seven-year-olds are dispersed throughout the school.

Vertical grouping is a very flexible arrangement. Each child can be placed in the group which suits him best and rarely are children from the same family placed together. School is the first chance a child has to get to know himself apart from his family and to gain a measure of independence. If the headmistress takes steps to get to know children before they are admitted, she can avoid obvious clashes of personality. As all teachers know, difficult children respond better to some adults than to others. If a child would benefit from a change of adult influence, teachers can suggest this.

A child can, however, stay with the same teacher for the span of his Infant School career. In this way teachers get to know their children very well and there is no break in the child's development. Educational continuity is particularly important during the first years of life. Even when the child is placed with the less gifted teacher, the emotional security of the stable environment she provides may be more important to the child than a sustained intellectual challenge.

This way of working demands more of teachers, but teachers enjoy being stretched. One teacher who changed to vertical grouping after thirty years of traditional teaching said, 'In all my experience I have never felt so near to my children. I go home exhausted every night, but I just couldn't change back.'

In a vertically grouped class children are learning at all levels, and whatever his age, level of ability, or stage of development, a child will find someone able to share his experiences. The more forward children set him standards to which he can aspire, whilst the children who are just beginning provide the satisfaction of showing him how far he has gone.

All teachers in a school grouped in this way share the same problems. A spirit of co-operation, rather than competition, fosters healthy working conditions. Miss Y, for instance, does not need to drive her children for fear of what Miss X will find when she gets them; Miss A cannot blame Mrs B for the gaps in her children's achievements. Each teacher carries the full responsibility of what happens to the child while he is in the Infant School. She has time to let the child develop from stage to stage more naturally. What he doesn't accomplish this year, he can cover in the next. In general, therefore, vertical grouping fosters family feeling throughout and the school works together as a unit.

Some teachers find this form of grouping a disadvantage during story time. On the whole, though, young children enjoy the story aimed a little beyond them and older children always welcome the repetition of stories they have enjoyed at a younger age. Provided that the atmosphere is maintained, is it always really necessary for every child to listen to the story?

Working together

Few teachers have solved the problem of integrating physical education into the child's working day. Here again vertical grouping may present snags. If, as in other fields, the work is largely on individual lines, the provision of sufficient apparatus should help to solve this problem.

We are not obliged to divide the school into class units, which persist mainly for purposes of registration. Although small children need the security of belonging to one person, there is no reason why all the children in the school shouldn't work together as a single community, with the full facilities of a team of teachers available to each child.

In many Infant Schools classroom doors stand open and there is much interchange between the classes. In some of the newer schools an open-plan type of building encourages flexible grouping. For example, Mrs Jones keeps a good supply of dolls' hair in her cupboard and will show a child how to sew it on. Miss Wilson knows a lot about electricity and she will help to fix the lighting-set in the puppet theatre. Mrs Bennett can give fine recipes to a child wanting to make cakes, and Mrs Tidy has been a nurse and knows what to do for a child who feels ill.

Liberal ways of working encourage us to experiment with organisation. In one old school a glass partition between classrooms is always open and three groups of children take advantage of a huge working area, with three teachers to whom they can apply for help. Then, towards the end of the day, the children settle into the comfort of the smaller group.

An even more extensive experiment in reorganisation is recommended in the Plowden Report, where we find the suggestion that First School should cater for children aged five to eight years and Middle School for children aged eight to twelve years. Some authorities have already planned to bring such reorganisation into effect. There is much to recommend grouping children within these age-ranges. Some twenty years ago, indeed, many Infant Schools kept children until the age of eight and were well aware of the benefits to the child of continuity during the first three years of his school education. The whole concept of transition from home to school and from school to school is reviewed in the Plowden Report, which firmly suggests that the law should allow for variations in practice so that the system can be made to fit the child.

However integrated the Infant School community may be, it does not provide education in isolation. The Infant School is a link between education in the Nursery years and what happens to the child in the Junior School. Its existence as a community is as a part of a total primary pattern.

The child entering school for the first time has extensive adjustments to make and these will be dealt with more fully in Chapters 11 and 12. We will concern ourselves here with ways in which links can be forged between home and school, and between Infant and Junior Schools.

At all stages adults associated with the child should know one another well and should know what happens to the child when he is in 'the other half of his world'. Many head teachers encourage parents to visit the school and to familiarise themselves with what goes on there before the child is admitted. In some cases a pre-school conference is arranged with parents.

Mass admission is avoided. A few children can be admitted each day in the first week of the term. In one school the headmistress admits before the term starts and the new entrants, with their mothers, have the run of the school for the day.

Children need not attend full-time during the first month or so. A day a week, or half-days, may ease a child into the community before he is formally registered. In some cases it is helpful to let Mother stay with her child in the classroom. Frequently it is the child who decides that the mother, who tends to cling to him, should go. He may be anxious to savour his first taste of independence, especially if Mother is possessive.

There are a number of tested ways in which good relationships between Infant and Junior Schools can be developed.

Working together

Teachers can follow their interest in the work of their colleagues by exchanging visits. Or the children due to be transferred can visit before the event, if only to sit in the classroom they will go to later and find out before the long holiday where to hang a cap on the first day. For the seven-year-old waiting those six weeks to go into the 'big' school, problems such as 'Will they know me?' 'Will there be a peg for my shoebag?' 'Who will I give my dinner money to?' can overshadow the coming event unless they are solved beforehand.

Occasionally a teacher may move up with a group of children and so provide continuity in their education. The staffs of some neighbouring Infant and Junior Schools meet at intervals over a cup of tea to discuss joint problems. They may run joint meetings with parents, or even a P.T.A. In one Infant School all the children knew and loved the headmaster of the Junior School and frequently went to him for help. The same children returned to their Infant School, perhaps for the morning service, from their elevated status as Juniors.

In the Infant Schools of today, teachers and children are not related to one another through organisation, or by certain methods and theories. They are living together, eager to share vital experiences. Life here is based on the nature of the child and upon the teacher's knowledge of the way in which he lives and grows and learns. All that happens here is in fact an expression of the truth that 'life educates'.

10

The integrated day

However the school is organised, we aim at creating an environment which will help the child to be himself and grow in his own way, and the teacher tries to arrange his day as naturally as possible.

The nature of the child and the way he views his world is crystallised in the words of Walt Whitman:

> There was a child went forth every day. [became,
> And the first object he looked upon, that object he
> And that object became part of him for the day,
> Or for many years or stretching cycles of years.

The timelessness of childhood, when time as the adult sees it means very little, allows the child to become lost in the wonder of what he finds and to remain absorbed until he has made each experience a part of himself. This is the mode of learning which comes naturally to him.

Does he need to wait in the playground until a bell rings or a door opens? In school there are many interesting jobs to do. Within reason, can he not come in and start work as soon as he arrives? If he chooses his own job he knows how to get on with it and can work independently, because he doesn't have to wait to be told what to do. He is answerable to the teacher even though she isn't physically present. He knows

The integrated day

that certain tools and materials are restricted unless she is present, and some head teachers feel that it is worth while taking the ultimate responsibility by allowing the child even this freedom.

Work that is interesting absorbs children so that they don't want to break off. When they change their jobs, they do so at different times and cannot be expected to complete a job just because the clock says ten o'clock, or time to change to another lesson. At the time when active programmes first gained recognition, many schools arranged set periods for number activities, reading and writing activities, creative activities and so on. In doing this they were imposing adult ideas of organisation on the children.

In practice, when children pursue their own interests activities overlap so much that these artificial divisions break down. The day is no longer an arrangement of clearly defined periods. It becomes a single span of time in which to work. It allows for integration of the child's various ways of learning.

The following example describes the experience of one teacher working in a school which was making the change from traditional to more informal ways of working.

'Creative play' in this school was a period on the timetable, taking place at the beginning of the day. It was followed by a period called the 3 R activities. In the 'creative play' period a group of boys converted an old milk-trolley into a bus. At pack-away time they were ready to put the bus on the road and wanted to make out a timetable for its journey. Instead of switching their attention to the work cards on 'the clock', which the teacher had prepared for them, she said they could carry on. By the end of the morning the boys had worked out a timetable at ten-minute intervals, had made tickets, a plan of the bus route and time sheets for the driver and the conductor.

'A real bus does sixty,' one boy observed. 'Ours only goes slow.'

Reaching out

The teacher felt satisfied about the ground covered in their enthusiasm and felt justified in letting them use the time in this way. They were showing her the value of being free to carry an interest through and treat the day as a single span of time.

Integration of the work develops as a result of the way in which the children are working and the concept the teacher has of her job. We can offer the child the opportunity to work in an absorbed and undivided way by providing long unbroken working periods, but integration does not happen simply because we decide it should. Where a school has worked for many years in traditional ways and with a fragmented timetable, the development of informal ways of working and of integration of the programme must come slowly and as a result of the growing confidence of the teacher in the child's ability to learn in ways natural to his individual growth as a person. In other words, if we have faith in our children as active agents of their own learning it is they who show us the need for work to be seen in terms of absorbing and wide-ranging interests, and it is they who effect a gradual change in classroom procedure.

A teacher who is interested in the idea of the integrated day has already started to provide for its development. She is obviously concerned about the way in which her children are learning and is prepared to expend effort on their behalf. Her sincere interest in their welfare helps to establish an atmosphere which is conducive to growth. She will need to follow this up in practical ways. She can start with the physical appearance of the classroom, both as regards the distribution of the furniture and the range and quality of material provided. Giving children long unbroken working periods in such a new-look classroom with little of value to do will lead to chaos. Likewise, giving them much of interest and leaving them in a classroom rigid with formally arranged furniture will again defeat her purpose.

The integrated day

It is unwise to remove familiar props too quickly. Some schools have made a start by leaving, say, the mornings free of timetable commitments. In other schools small groups of children are allowed to pursue unbroken interests, although it is found that these groups tend to work in limited ways when the rest of the class is following a traditional timetable.

Imaginative materials and vital situations are the most effective agents of integration. If we provide the child with what absorbs and satisfies him, he will prove to us the need to work with few interruptions and the increased value to him of what he learns. It is in this way that teachers gain confidence in freeing children to learn fully from what we offer, instead of learning only within the limits of the work we direct them to do. Where teachers have come to believe in these basic principles of learning, education in the school becomes a dynamic force, adjusting to the ever-varying needs of children, and the way we work today is not necessarily the way we shall work tomorrow.

Even playtime breaks have disappeared in many schools. The children themselves have dispensed with them.

'Must we leave the bird-table we're making just when we're getting the top to stay on?' 'I don't want to go into the playground. There's nothing to do there and I'm in the middle of writing a most exciting story.'

Where so-called playtime breaks have disappeared, so have many of those minor accidents. In fact, the only breaks we really need in the day are for the use of the hall or of the climbing apparatus, and for the school service and dinner-time. This does not mean that the teacher needs to forgo her well-earned coffee and tea breaks; it is important, in fact, that teachers should gather together from time to time during the day, for such informal staff meetings are essential to the mental health of the school. If the classroom work is well organised, children can manage without the teacher for a short time; indeed in one classroom children used to set the alarm to warn the teacher when it was her coffee break. When children are responsible for the job they are doing, they can work without the full-time direct supervision of the teacher, for the spirit of her discipline is maintained even when she is not there.

We have considered the range of experiences a teacher needs to provide in the classroom. How do all these fit together? Work is now thought of in terms of activities, rather than separate subjects, and the job the child chooses can include as much creative as academic work, so that, in the classroom, the teacher thinks in terms of real-life situations rather than subject-bound periods.

Few classrooms are designed to cater for modern methods, and much depends on the ingenuity of the teacher. The floor space needs to be broken up into a number of working bays. A cupboard, for instance, set at right angles to the wall, can provide shelves on one side, while slats of wood nailed across the back, with curtain wires above, will display books. Simple open dividers which provide display shelves, the position of desks, book racks and even the trolley of waste materials can suggest divisions of space which add interest to the room and separate the main activities.

Children need space if they are to work and move freely without friction, and we should dispense with as much furniture as possible. Do we really need one chair per child? Can working surfaces, engineered by moving tables together, replace the desk-per-child arrangement? The teacher's desk takes up less room if the top is used by the children, and if cupboard doors are removed much valuable space is gained.

In our anxiety to include everything we must avoid cluttering the environment; there must be somewhere for the eye to rest without being stimulated. The dangers of over-stimulation should not be forgotten and there should be serenity in a child's day and a place for meditation.

A general principle in planning a room is to organise it so that only a few children work in any one part at one time;

The integrated day

no more than four children need use clay, or paint, or do woodwork at the same time, and learning to take turns is part of their social training.

If children are to work happily in a free atmosphere they need the security of good planning and organisation. The success of an informal approach depends considerably on the discipline behind it. A clear understanding between teacher and children as to how the classroom is run for the benefit of all is essential, and each child should be taught to put back materials and tools in the right place after use; thus, when John has finished making his clay man, he will hang his rubber apron where he knows the next child can find it. The preparation of paint and paste is part of their work. The children, not the caretaker or the teacher, should be responsible for the orderly care of the classroom, and although it may take weeks to educate children into the classroom habits expected of them, these are weeks well spent.

Children should be encouraged to explore beyond the confines of their classroom. In corners of the hall or along corridors they may find equipment, perhaps of a more expensive nature, which is available to the whole school: for example, displays of objects from other countries, a selection of things made from wood or glass, the more valuable books, musical or mathematical instruments A pet corner and a vivarium both offer interests which enable children to meet and discuss with children from other classes.

In one school a permanent milk bar, organised and run by the children, is situated in a corner of a corridor behind the steps leading up to the hall, and here children from all classes take their milk at any time during the day. Another teacher may prefer to have a classroom milk bar, and may wish to keep it open only during the morning. Labels, bearing the name of each child in the class, are slipped over the bottles when they arrive and it is simple to check in this way who has or has not had milk. The social training here is considerable.

Reaching out

The classroom is the child's workshop and in it he will learn to live as one of a community; he will discover himself as a person and will be free to experiment, to make mistakes and to learn from them.

Planning a classroom in this way means that the child's learning can be continuous and integrated. An example of the work done by a group of children in a vertically grouped school which planned for an integrated day may help to illustrate some of the points made.

An unusually sunny September stimulated observation of the sun. One group of four six-year-old boys became fascinated by its journey through space. They noticed that 'there were other things in the space round the earth. There were stars and a moon.'

An older boy explained 'things in the sky' to one of the group. He fetched a book on astronomy from the library corner in the hall to illustrate his points. Thereafter the book on astronomy was fetched by one or other of the boys each day. Distances in miles of planets from the earth filled the boys with awe. Whilst unable to understand such distances, they were able to grasp some notion of the immensity of space.

They constructed a 'space' using a hoop. The sun was suspended from the centre of the hoop. Planets made from crushed paper were suspended in relative positions.

The boys described their experiences at home and one mother invited the group to view on her television set a senior science programme on space. The boys were allowed to go to the home at 2.20 p.m. Soon after 3 p.m. they burst into the classroom full of information. With help from the teacher and the older boy they wrote up their impressions of the programme with illustrations.

Margaret, aged four-and-a-half, showed interest in these activities from the start. She watched the boys at work and heard their comments. While they were reading the book they had made to the rest of the class and some of the teachers, she went to the painting corner and painted a picture which she called 'Space'. It was a seething mass of swirling black and purple. 'It's a tunnel,' she explained. 'It's the space in a tunnel when the train's gone through.'

This example illustrates the balance between individual and group participation. At some points children were working alone, at others a small group shared a common interest and from time to time the whole class became involved.

Exploration often arises from the spontaneous interests of the child, but interests initiated by the teacher can be equally rewarding. The balance between teacher-initiated activity and activity arising from the spontaneous interests of children is not easy to determine.

In the following situation the initial interest was activated by material produced by the teacher.

One teacher was particularly appreciative of wood. She had collected from time to time a wide variety of objects made from wood and many natural examples of wood in its various forms. Her most treasured possession was a wooden bowl her father had carved from oak. It was beautifully made and polished to display the flower of the grain. She decided to share her pleasure with the children and during a collective period at the end of the day she showed them the bowl.

They responded to her appreciative handling of the bowl and began to chatter about things made from wood. The next morning when they arrived they found a display of 'Wood'. It contained the bark from various trees, a log of pinewood, samples of many kinds of wood and pieces of veneer, a beautifully shaped wooden spoon from Sweden, an Indian ring box made from sandal-wood, a carved cherry-wood statue from Japan, a baby's rattle made in teak, a spinning-wheel, an old cart-wheel made from wood bound by an iron rim, a cider barrel and a rocking chair put together without nails.

The children handled these objects and asked questions. The teacher answered some of them, but more often she

Reaching out

referred the questioner to the reference books she had arranged near by. She knew a lot about her material and was able to lead the children on in their curiosity and interest.

By the end of the day a number of areas of discovery were established. One group of five-year-old children were comparing the floating quality of various woods. Another group were trying to find out how they could spin real wool and make some cloth. Others wanted to know what cider was and were planning to make some with cooking apples. A number had turned to the woodwork bench with fresh inspiration, while one child painted a pattern clearly inspired by the grain of the oak in the bowl.

From time to time in the days which followed the children added to the teacher's display things they brought from home and things they made themselves. They were helped to display these things attractively and to treat them with respect. They were learning in many ways through their various interests, but these interests originated in the teacher's own enthusiasm. Work of this kind, where teachers and children are free of unnecessary restrictions, opens up unexpected sources of discovery for both teacher and children.

11

Home and school

The child's home background and his medical history are closely related to the work we do with him in school.[24] He is part of a family and the provision we make for him in school must be seen as part of his total environment. The education of the whole child calls for co-operation between parents and teachers, and a child cannot develop as he should if school and home are separated worlds, for his home life and his school life together create his living day.[25] Hostility between the two has a very detrimental effect on a child's mental health. The following extract from a teacher's record book illustrates the importance of communication between home and school.

'From the start David has been a very difficult child in school. Indoors he just sits and will not join in any of the activities, but out in the playground he chases wildly around, calling at the top of his voice. Not until half way through the year did David admit to having a sister. His mother tells me that in his early years David played an unfortunate role in the family. His parents lived with Grandmother and Grandfather. Grandmother was an invalid, and was given constant attention by David's mother. Both grandparents died and soon after David's sister was born.'

The sympathetic understanding engendered by such

Reaching out

information gives support to the teacher in handling the child, and it fosters in her a helpful attitude towards him.

It is not always easy to enlist the co-operation of parents. Some parents tend to be aggressive.

'I don't hold with this cardboard packet education. Why, our Susan does nothing but enjoy herself all day. In my day we had to work hard. We hated school, but it learnt us.'

Other parents abdicate. This note, written on an empty sugar bag, was sent to a head teacher:

'Our Steve (age seven) stole a bob from his mum's purse. It's happened afore. Pleas see as he don't do it agen. We've done wi him.'

We need to build up the confidence of such parents, both in themselves and in what we are attempting. They need to know that their children are our joint concern. Their children are our guests, and between us we help them to grow. Parents often fear the unfamiliar.

If we keep them out of school – 'No parents allowed beyond this gate' – and if we shroud our methods in secrecy, they attack because they don't understand. We can welcome them into the school and reassure them of our sincere concern for their children.

An organised parent–teacher association, which devotes much of its energy to providing out-of-school social contact, is not always the best means of helping children. Children need to see their parents and teachers working together on their behalf. The more informal such contact is, the better. In some schools parents are invited to visit during school hours at regular intervals; each week the parents of one class can be invited to visit their children in school for the last part of the afternoon, whilst the children carry on with their normal jobs as far as possible. Parents can then see what is happening, and be encouraged to ask questions to which they receive adequate replies and explanations. As only one class at a time is involved, the head teacher can be present to discuss the general policy of the school.

Home and school

This arrangement provides opportunity for the teacher to discover factors in the child's home background which influence his behaviour in school. Parents, seeing their own child in relationship to others of similar age, can take a more objective and balanced view of him. The children are desperately anxious to have Mother and Father see what they do in school. With the help of the teacher, each child can write his own invitation, and woe betide the parent who doesn't turn up, or at least send a representative! Sometimes the teacher can display on a table the kind of material helpful parents can supply, such as an old wireless set or discarded wheels and other examples of interesting waste. When parents feel they are contributing to the work of the school in ways such as these, they turn their attention to helping solve problems rather than look for mistakes.

Another advantage of this procedure is the fact that Mother brings the pre-school-age children with her. Right from his pram stage the future pupil is familiar with school and sees it as an exciting part of his future.

Parents attending in this way watch their child's progress from its small beginnings. They feel involved in what the school is attempting and they are anxious to help when their interest is evoked and respected. They see their children are happy and this gives them confidence in the teacher. Informal relationship of this kind is much more valuable than formal Open Days, concerts, and the like. Sometimes larger groups of parents and friends participate in a carol service or a spring festival, when teachers, parents, children and friends of the school share in the rejoicing. This is educationally sound, whereas much time can be wasted in training children to perform to an audience.

There are times when school policy can be more freely discussed if the children are not present. An evening meeting, when fathers have a better opportunity to attend, can be held perhaps once a year. In one school the agenda took the form of questions submitted by parents. The headmistress and her staff were supported by the local schools' organiser in their replies and in the discussion which developed.

It is often the parent we most wish to meet who avoids meetings of this kind. A personal letter from the head teacher may help: 'Something seems to be holding David back. He lacks confidence in his work and finds it difficult to make friends. I am sure you can help us to understand David's problem and I shall look out for you particularly on Parents' Afternoon.'

A note to the manager of the local factory where many of the mothers may work will often persuade him to release them for an hour on the appropriate afternoon. Some parents may be free only in the evening and it may be possible to arrange a later session for them. It is essential to involve every parent, and efforts to do so are very well rewarded.

It is helpful, too, to enlist the interest of parents when making changes in school policy. For instance, a school wishing to reorganise and become vertically grouped could invite parents to discuss changes as they affect their children, in advance. In so doing we avoid misunderstandings on the part of parents and no one wonders, for example, why 'my Gloria' has gone up, or down, as the case may be. When embarking on new ventures we must expect to make some mistakes and parents are less likely to lose confidence if these possibilities have been discussed in advance.

The Plowden Report emphasises the importance of this close partnership between the home and the school, and sees it as essential to educational advance. The report suggests not only that parents should be welcomed into the school and involved in its activities, but that they should be kept well informed about educational developments and that the school should remain open beyond the ordinary school hours for the use of the community. Some schools have already organised clubs in holiday times and in out-of-school hours, when parents

Home and school

and teachers provide activities for children and for adults. Chapter 4 of the Report contains some excellent suggestions for future developments in building up good relations between schools and parents.

We have considered ways in which the link can be made between school and home before children are registered and we have dealt with organised meetings. These are not by any means the only form of contact. Each day offers many incidental opportunities for developing good relationships with parents.

The school medical or dental examination provides excellent contact. Parents and teachers are on mutual ground with a third person present who offers an objective view of the child. Obvious physical concern for a child often speaks more clearly to parents than concern for emotional and intellectual development. Often, of course, a physical defect is closely associated with other problems. Terry, for instance, tried to avoid physical education when he could. A medical examination revealed a minor foot deformity which worried Terry when he wore plimsolls, and the unnatural resistance to physical activity no longer puzzled his teacher.

Day-to-day incidents may provide just the right opening or opportunity to visit the home of a child. Derek, for instance, was a constant source of worry to his teacher. He was undersized and peaky with hands like the frail claws of a sparrow. He took sweets, biscuits, toys and pennies from children's pockets and he would be found lurking amongst the coats in the cloakroom. One day he brought two shillings for bank stamps and went home at night without claiming his bank book. The teacher called at the house with the book.

'I thought you might worry and think Derek had lost it on the way home,' she explained to the mother. The mother was shaken. She had given Derek no money for stamps. The teacher found out in the end that Derek was an adopted child who remembered the mother who left him in a children's home.

Reaching out

Petty theft was a means of compensating himself for the loss of his mother's love. This was an emotional problem and, working together, foster-mother and teacher were able to help him.

In the following story we see how a good relationship between teacher and parents helped two little girls with similar problems to make adjustments and become happier children. Jane was extremely quiet when she started school. She spent much of her time by herself, drawing. Even in story time she sat apart and her teacher found great difficulty in communicating with her. Occasionally she would play with other little girls, but got very excited and spoilt the play. She avoided boys completely.

Claire was in the same class. She cried easily and very poor speech made it difficult for her to communicate with other children. She would run to her older sister, who was also in the school, when she was upset.

On parents' visiting day the teacher talked to both mothers. She discovered that Jane complained at home that no one would play with her. Mother explained that there was an older and a younger brother and that Jane seemed to resent them and this might account for her attitude to boys in school. Claire's mother said that a very lively young sister had taken up much of her time and she felt she'd neglected Claire. She said Claire lacked confidence and they'd taken her to a speech therapist who said that her speech would improve.

The teacher encouraged the two little girls to work together. She gave them similar jobs to do, making sure that less was demanded of Claire. Whenever possible she helped them to share some responsibility with other children. When Claire was six her mother let her give a birthday party to which Jane was invited, along with other little girls in the class. Friendships became established for both little girls and Claire gained confidence.

Claire's speech began to improve and she started to read.

Although Jane continued to avoid boys she became more talkative and mixed with other children more easily. Rather tempestuous friendships ensued and once-silent children grew noisy. Their happy faces amply compensated their teacher, who said of them, 'They are more excitable and sometimes hard to control. Their voices are often strident, but friendship is such an exciting experience and their happy faces make it worth all the extra work they now give me.'

12

The mental health of the child

The mental health of an individual depends on the opportunity he has for the full expression of himself as a person. Personal fulfilment is usually accompanied by happiness, and happiness in a child is a sign that what he is doing is bringing him satisfaction. Positive attitudes to life help a person to make satisfactory adjustments. The child who learns to view the world as a place which is full of opportunity and interest and as a place where he can make full contribution as the person he is, will be in a much better position than the child who learns to fear the world, distrust the people he meets in it and doubt his ability to cope with it.

There is much a teacher can do to help a child to feel in harmony with his surroundings, and healthy mental development in school depends on at least three important factors. First, the child must feel accepted as he is, the good with the bad. Second, the child must find in school recognition of his needs as an individual. Third, the quality of relationships which exist in the school community should enable him to learn from other personalities. The teacher herself provides the link between him and the experiences offered in school.

School is the child's first step into that vast community beyond his home. For many children, however well prepared they may be, it is a very terrifying experience to leave home behind and part with Mother. One of the first jobs the teacher has to do is to help the child to develop a sense of immediacy. When Mother leaves the child and disappears, it's no good telling him that she's gone home to cook his dinner and he'll see her at lunchtime; he has to learn by sheer experience that Mother can be with him in spirit even though she is not with him physically. This sense of the nearness of loved ones is something which supports us through the whole of our lives; learning how to part with those who are dearest to us is one of the first things an Infant teacher has to help a child to do. Patience and comfort help to a certain extent, but enabling the child to become absorbed through interest helps even more. If we can offer him something in the environment which catches him up completely and takes his mind off himself, he discovers much to his amazement that although Mother has departed he has not missed her and nothing unpleasant has happened to him.

Once the child has become to a certain extent independent of his family, he must feel accepted in the new community. Integration of the personality depends on self-acceptance.[26] A child can only dare to be himself, to become himself, when he likes what he knows of that self. The child who is made to feel acceptable to the teacher he admires and to the other children on whom he depends for friendship is in a better position to accept himself and make a job of being himself than the child who is only accepted in those parts of him that please the teacher and rejected for those things which annoy her. A teacher may disapprove of a child's unkempt appearance or his unfortunate behaviour, but if she can accept these things as part of what the child is, she can help the child to improve matters. If she makes him feel inferior and unwanted, he will live up to the idea she has of him and become what she obviously thinks he is.

Sometimes what the child is disturbs us. Anti-social behaviour, for instance, is difficult to accept. It isn't the normally naughty child, however, who is the teacher's real problem. The docile child may not be a nuisance to us; the child who is excessively tidy and the child who is desperately anxious to be clever or good often evoke our warm approval, but this kind of behaviour can indicate incipient neurosis and can be just as disturbing as bed-wetting, bullying, stealing, lying, biting and other forms of anti-social behaviour.[27]

The pattern of harmonious relationships in school depends considerably on the kind of discipline which holds the group together. Freedom in the modern Infant School has sometimes been misinterpreted as licence. Children need the security of a framework of discipline they understand.[28] Freedom means freedom of choice within certain limits. We expect children at this stage to be immature in many ways. They have much to learn about the balance between their own desires and the needs of others. They frequently present the teacher with behaviour problems. While we should avoid imposing adult standards of behaviour on young children, we must be realistic in our attitude to discipline if we are to allow children to develop in their individual ways. Discipline which stems from the child's own motivation is of greater value to him than that imposed by adults.

By freedom, we mean a wide but not unlimited freedom of choice. When the teacher equips the environment, she has already guided the child in his choice of activity. Knowing her children, she guides each one of them into selecting a job within his capacity, but the child is free to select a job which interests him. It is his job and he is now responsible for seeing it through; he wants to do it well and he will concentrate in his efforts to satisfy himself. He can plan for himself, because he knows what he wants to do – he doesn't have to wait to be told by the teacher what to do next. When his job creates problems which are too great for him he can apply to his teacher for help, but for much of the time he is independent and may even forget that the teacher is there.

The mental health of the child

The child's self-chosen job is important to him and his attention is fixed on it: this is real concentration and he has no time to waste on anti-social behaviour. This is also discipline. The freedom of choice and the discipline of the chosen task create the atmosphere for active methods of teaching.

The teacher, too, is involved in this kind of discipline. The child chooses his job; the teacher ensures that he fulfils his responsibility and completes his task to the best of his ability.

Geoffrey was academically weak, but he was interested in knitting and completed a square for the blanket which was to be sent to the refugees. He then said he would like to make a book about his knitting, so the teacher stapled a few pages together for him, using as the cover the piece of pink card he had chosen himself.

Ten minutes later the teacher found Geoffrey's book. On the first page there was a drawing the size of a pea and a bit of scribble in one corner. Geoffrey was missing. She found him watching the rabbits. 'I couldn't write "knitting",' Geoffrey complained.

'You know what to do if you want help with a word,' she reminded him. 'I made the book for you with a piece of my best card. We agreed, didn't we, that you would write it all down? I will help you and we'll do a page each day until it's finished.' Geoffrey was extremely proud of his book when it was finished and kept it to show Mother on visiting day.

When we accept children and encourage them to be individuals we increase our problems, for when children are not expected to conform to a recognised pattern their individual differences and characteristics become emphasised. We see them as they really are, the good with the bad. We develop their assets and at the same time we give them the opportunity to exhibit their idiosyncrasies. The flexible environment we provide gives us a good deal of scope for dealing with problems and helping children to solve them.

Extracts from records kept by teachers will illustrate some

Reaching out

of the problems we are likely to meet in children and how one person has dealt with them.

The first example consists of a series of records made by a reception class teacher who received the three children concerned from the same family at yearly intervals.

'Mother was a doctor before marriage. She is an austere and highly intelligent woman. Child-bearing has not softened her and she regards her well-built children as a biological achievement on her part. Father travels away from home for long periods on business and never comes near the school, even on open evenings.

'When the first child, a girl, came into school she clung persistently to my skirt. She cried easily and perpetually insisted "Come and look at my . . ." She drew immature "octopus" figures and chattered incessantly. When biscuits were on sale she became very aggressive, because Mother never gave her a penny (a child shouldn't eat between meals).

'She "stole" small items, e.g. chalk, sweets, a piece of ribbon and, later, money from the dinner tin. Mother was quite sure that her child couldn't possibly do such a thing. I talked very gently to Mother, but didn't get very far.

'The second child, a boy, was tall for his age and over-powering. He was highly excitable. Beads of perspiration broke out on his lip when he tried to express himself. In dramatic play his excitability swamped other children and they stared at him in silence. Sometimes I asked him to come and help play the piano (lower keys) to calm him down.

'I found him one day scrabbling in the biscuit tin. He was stuffing the contents down his throat, and crumbs covered his coat and the floor. He took children's money and biscuits. When told of this, Mother was less certain of his innocence and, later, began to tell me of the "crimes" he committed at home. "Is he a good boy in school? You don't know what he did . . ."

'The third child, a girl, was much quieter and rather a

pleasant child. She was accepted by the group, but even she "took" the odd treasure. Now, however, Mother made her return even the smallest item she took home from school.

'Circumstances have forced Mother to modify her attitude towards the behaviour of her children. She even feels guilty, but still refuses to admit any physical faults in her children. When the older girl was taken home one day following a fall, Mother said firmly, "She can walk. There is nothing wrong with her."

'If only I could get Mother to let her children be just ordinary children it would help, but I feel she has never made them feel wanted for themselves and they can never become really sensitive to others.'

In spite of her efforts, the teacher realised the limitations of her position. The very powerful influence of parental attitude is clearly evident.

The following illustrations relate to seven-year-old children who were slow to learn. In both cases, for different reasons, the child suffered from linguistic difficulties, and we see the close relationship between the child's personal confidence and his ability to succeed at school.

'Roy suffers from being the less able and less forceful twin, and from being the only boy amongst three girls of strong character. He had a very marked stutter when he first came into school. Separated from his twin sister he has made rapid progress, particularly in reading. A certain amount of success has given him confidence and his stutter is less marked . . .'

'Timothy suffers from deafness, which varies in degree. When Timothy has a cold he is very deaf. When he came into school at the beginning of the year, he was completely lacking in confidence. He had a slight stutter which has improved during the year. He is intelligent, but lack of success in his work and an inability to mix with others have made life difficult for him. When able to produce a good piece of work, his face lights up with the praise that is given him. I give him small jobs which make him feel responsible and the importance this gives him is helping to build up his confidence.'

In these ways we are reminded constantly of the interrelated nature of the child's growth and learning. Deficiencies in any aspect of the child's life, whether it be deafness or enuresis, an unsatisfactory role in the family group, a faulty relationship or a poor physical environment, lead to disturbance of personal growth. Emotional health along with all other aspects of the child is dependent on complete and satisfactory development.

Central to the child's environment is his teacher. What she is as a person matters more than anything else. In her the child needs to find integrity and that harmony of the person which supports her under all circumstances. Many of our children come from homes where adults live in a state of conflict. There is little harmony in their lives and they depend on their teacher for a measure of serenity. Sometimes, for a child just to be near a quiet person is in itself enough. The most positive contribution the teacher can make to the mental health of the child is to be the right kind of human being, possessing an inner serenity which helps to establish a balanced emotional climate for the children who depend on her.

13

The gifted child and the slow learner

Some of the teacher's most searching problems are associated with children who learn at abnormal rates. The gifted child and the slow learner have much in common. Both would seem to pass through normal stages; where they differ from the norm is in rate, not sequence.

From the earliest days it is evident that children learn at different rates, but the effects of this become more apparent each year. As the gifted child or the slow learner works through the Primary School and into the Secondary School, the gap between him and the normal learner widens. We shall, therefore, refer frequently in this chapter to the problems confronting the child during his later Primary School days, when the effects of abnormal rates of learning become more clearly established.

It is customary in our educational system to use the concept of intelligence as our main criterion in determining whether a child is normal, gifted, or backward. Measurements of intelligence tend to stress scholastic attainment, yet it is obviously difficult to separate personality and even physical development from the concept of intelligence.[29]

In order to understand the learning problems presented by the gifted and the backward, we need to have a clear idea of what we mean by intelligence and how the provision made for the child in school can affect its development. Intelligence is not a power we can measure, we can only measure the effects of it in terms of differences in performance; and the child's capacity to reason, to benefit from past experience and to perceive relationships, is accepted as evidence of intellectual capacity.

The relative importance of heredity and environment has been debated for centuries. Certainly at birth the blueprint of future development is established, but the environment before, during and after birth plays a vital part in the attainment of that potential. Comparatively little is known about the brain, but we know that it does not develop as it should if it is starved of stimulation and that the development of intellectual capacity depends on the brain. Effective sense organs feed information to the brain and provide the link between the environment and the mind. Interest also plays an important part and intelligence moves along paths which are closely associated with our interests.

Intelligence tests, by and large, measure differences in verbal performance. Even non-verbal intelligence tests require the capacity to think out relationships or 'talk to ourselves' and internalise language, and so are linguistically based.[30] Recent trends towards open-ended tests should minimise the handicap of the creative child whose answers do not conform to the general pattern, but assessment of these tests at the moment is far from reliable.

Experienced teachers are quick to recognise intelligence even in very young children whose language is still immature. The way a child responds to a question or simple instruction, the way in which he makes relationships or solves his problems, are very good guides. The very appearance of the child provides many clues. Interest, curiosity and understanding are easily detected in the child's expression, but it is the child's use of words, even in the earliest stages, which is our most reliable guide.

The idea of intelligence remaining fixed and unalterable is no longer held. We know that within certain limits it can be improved, but research confirms a ceiling to this improvement.[31] We know, for instance, that a young child of low intelligence can make outstanding improvement in a stimulating environment coupled with care and affection. Similarly the highly intelligent child may not reach his full potential if his environment is arid or unsympathetic, or if he feels different and unacceptable.

A literate society demands literacy from its members if they are to succeed, and in our educational system academic attainments, particularly the skill of reading, are considered very important. The days when the rich farmer signed his cheques with a cross are gone.

We demand more of the child between seven and fourteen, and here we find the greatest number of backward individuals. After that the percentage diminishes and backwardness has been called by Penrose 'a self-curing disease'.[32] In other words, the child is only considered backward because his pace is slower than others. Given time many would reach a socially effective level.

Although a child's development in the educational system is normally classified according to academic attainment, we could use other criteria. A child could be said to be physically gifted or retarded. We could assess him socially and emotionally, or creatively, or mechanically. We could define four types of intelligence – verbal, mechanical, social and creative. Many children seem to be gifted or slow in a general sense, so that some seem to have all the gifts and others very few.

The interaction of physical and mental development is all-important in the development of personality, and we know how personality affects total development. How does it feel to be behind all one's classmates? How do you fit in when you know all the answers and are ahead of the teacher, let alone father and mother?

What of the child who is gifted in some special way: a brilliant pianist, say, and yet unable to cope with normal classroom activities? What of the budding poet who will be expected to 'do English grammar', or the ingenious child who craves to invent and who will be required to copy down notes about the science experiment the teacher demonstrated? These children don't fit in and our examination system doesn't assess them. They need our understanding and should not be made to conform to our idea of the normal pattern.

We need to know as soon as possible that children are backward or brilliant. We need to accept them as members of the group and yet provide facilities for their own particular requirements. They need understanding parents, understanding teachers, and suitable methods and materials to alleviate emotional as well as intellectual difficulties.

A child is classified as backward because he is a slow learner. By this we mean that he learns at a slower rate than the norm of the group, and in any group of people there are bound to be some at this end of the scale. The child's slowness, then, is a relative term.

The child's rate of learning may be slow for a number of reasons. His intellectual capacity may be limited. He may suffer from some physical defect. Impairment of any of his senses slows up his rate of learning. He may lack muscular co-ordination. The defect, physical or motor, may have been caused before, during, or after birth. The effects of anoxia (oxygen imbalance) during birth, for instance, may affect the efficiency of the brain.[33] Research on the effects of oxygen supply to the baby, before or after birth, opens up a number of possibilities. Even an accident in early childhood can hinder normal development.

Most teachers have met children with an emotional blockage. Poor relationships with people the child depends on are often at the root of such problems. Bowlby emphasises the extreme importance of the childs' relationship with his mother.[34] In

The gifted child and the slow learner

school a child may clash temperamentally with his teacher. One of the advantages of flexible grouping, such as vertical grouping, is the opportunity for placing a child in a suitable social situation. Even in helpful circumstances a child may be absent from school at a critical period and the opportune moment for helping an aptitude or skill to develop may be missed. If he has missed a vital step in his learning, he may be unable to bridge the gap. Without skilful help this can start a chain of worsening effects, with the child slipping further and further behind his classmates.

A child may be born into an environment which offers him little chance of fulfilment. He may inherit an overcrowded home where the level of subsistence is low and there is little order, or where parents are cruel to their children, often through ignorance – the 'submerged tenth' our sociologists talk about. Can we expect a child to make academic progress when there are no books in the home and when the values and attitudes of parents are in conflict with the aims and values of the school?[35]

Our slow learner may lack even an illiterate home; he may have been institutionalised from an early age. Increasing awareness of the vital necessity for the young child to identify with a mother figure has revolutionised our orphanages, but much remains to be done.

Whatever the cause of the child's apparent inability to learn normally, his slower pace must be accepted. Drilling the child into performing mechanical tricks in arithmetic, for instance, will not help him to understand. He needs the stimulation of a vital environment yet with time for consolidation, for reflection, for assimilation. Hurrying will hinder the development of difficult processes such as reading and numbering. Although early diagnosis is essential, we must give these children the chance to develop amongst normal children and we avoid separating them before the age of seven. Some slow-learning children need special treatment if they are to learn to fit into society, but many of our slow learners can be educated more adequately by belonging to normal groups. They learn much from normal children and would suffer if placed in schools for the educationally subnormal.

Perhaps their most desperate need is to acquire the skill of reading. The youth who is unable to read notices at work, to fill in his own football pools, to read the destination and number of a bus, is at a serious disadvantage socially and emotionally. The heavyweight boxer may succeed in his profession with little reading until he wants to write to his girl friend. During the war years classes in basic reading were exceptionally well attended by those in the Forces who wished to correspond with home. Failure to read in our society is demoralising.

It is natural for parents to want their children to pass through the normal stages of development at roughly the correct time. Some parents indeed are fanatic about this and their attitudes do not help the slower child. He needs extra understanding from parents and later from teachers. These teachers need to be more than loving, caring people; they need the mental stability to cope with the demands and failures of these children, together with the skill to diagnose reasons for failure and to devise ways of helping them to win through.

Not all backward children come from down-town homes. We find the slower learner in every type of home, and it is sometimes said that the prospects of the child from the good home environment are less favourable than those for a similar child with a poor home environment. The child in the good home, it would seem, has failed in spite of every chance and we have little more to offer him.

Some slower learning children come from homes which are materially good, where parents lavish money, sweets, toys and clothes on their children, but deny them the warmth of love and affection. Julia was well clothed and fed. She had expensive toys and a real leather satchel to carry her plimsolls to school. Her only claim to success was the approval she bought from her classmates with sweets and chocolate. They accepted her gifts, even included her in some of their games, but their friendship was fickle, based on very shaky foundations, and she hadn't a personal friend amongst them.

Marianne always looked most attractive. Her expensive little dresses and pretty hair style gave her a superficial brightness which was very misleading. At eleven, she could scarcely read because no one had considered her for remedial teaching. It seemed impossible to believe that she could be dull.

At the age of nine, George was recommended for a remedial class. His father, a solicitor, was furious and objected vociferously to such treatment for his son. An understanding teacher managed to persuade him of George's problems. Ultimate success in reading proved the accuracy of the diagnosis and reinstated George in his father's eyes.

These are exceptions and the majority of backward children come from under-privileged homes and lack the vital spark or motivation to succeed academically.

Tony lived in a culturally arid home on a housing estate. He was undersized and seemed utterly bewildered by all that went on around him. He was exceptionally slow and never finished his work. His inability to read didn't worry him very much. There were no books at home and he wasn't used to seeing adults enjoy reading. Tony was a pleasant boy. He made friends with a more intelligent child and this friendship became an important factor in his development, providing him with emotional stability and challenge. His efforts became more purposeful and he developed a sense of pride in his work.

Given helpful conditions, time, and a sympathetic teacher, children like Tony can at least learn to read and so lead an adequate life in a literate society. They ought never to enter the Secondary School labelled as failures and there become fearful and joyless or aggressive and rebellious, with delinquency as their ultimate destiny. If society fails them their only mode of expression is to turn against it, and we can prevent this happening if we wish.

Clearly linguistic skill is an index of intelligence. At the other end of the normal range we find the gifted child who is frequently superior in physique as well as being highly intelligent. Many have special gifts. Almost invariably they are gifted linguistically, with culturally good homes which encourage the development of initial high intelligence. They communicate freely with others and reason their way through problems.

A child with a special skill, such as a gift for music, may not fit in with the ideas his parents have for him. The examination system in school doesn't cater for him. He may become withdrawn and even deprived socially and emotionally and, eventually, linguistically. Some parents do not approve of a daughter who enjoys mathematics but has little interest in make-up and clothes, or the son who prefers books to football. Such parents may want their offspring to become socially successful, and growing up for these children may present great problems.

Gifted children are often extremely sensitive. They easily feel misunderstood when parents and teachers show indifference to their gifts. Some adults remain unaware of what such children can offer. They may even fear what they do not understand. A gifted child can be an intellectual threat to a teacher, who may fail to see that she can help the child who is more intelligent than herself and that there is great joy for herself in doing so. Some teachers may even feel jealous of the child who should ultimately hold a high position in society. It takes a mature person to rejoice in the academic achievements of others.

Many of these gifted children become desperately unhappy through lack of understanding and their gifts are lost to society. But the loss to the child in terms of his happiness is enormous if he is forced to hide his talents, instead of being encouraged to exploit them. If he knows all the answers he can be unpopular. Sometimes a gifted child will strengthen his feeling of belonging by appearing to be no better than his friends.

Lynda, an attractive girl of nine, was physically and intellectually gifted. She was also highly imaginative and could easily get caught up in the world of her imagination. She was happy when left to her own devices, but she enjoyed the companionship of other children too and she didn't always get it. One day a group of girls were playing 'hospitals' and Lynda wasn't invited to join them.

'Why don't they choose me?' she asked her teacher. 'I love being a nurse and I know all about injections and things.'

The teacher seized an opportunity to ask the other girls and was told, 'Lynda doesn't play our games', and 'She talks like a book and we don't know what she means'. These children were simply not able to keep pace with Lynda in thought. Lynda learned to shrug her shoulders and retreat to her world of books where she felt safe.

Susan was linguistically gifted. She loved words and wrote wonderful poetry, but she did not perform well in the 11-plus and her gifts wilted as the State system closed against her. David, with musical talent, was sent by worshipful parents to a school ten miles from his home for musically gifted children. He grew away from the children who lived near his home and it was difficult to maintain friendship with the children he met in school. Eventually his gift for music deteriorated and he left school a very ordinary boy with few friends.

These children need the opportunity to explore their gifts and develop them, they need the challenge of minds as sharp as their own, but they are still children and they need to grow socially and emotionally within a normal group if they are to become whole in personality. They desperately need to be loved, accepted and respected for what they are. Within recent years more attention has been paid to these gifted children. At one time teachers thought they 'could get on by themselves', or that 'they were precocious and needed a healthy dose of neglect'. Today television, radio and the press recognise the problem posed by these children to parents and teachers. The activities of the Association for Gifted Children enable parents to get together and come to terms with the problem of helping these children to offer their gifts to society. Acceptance and the full understanding of teachers and parents are the first steps towards integrating these children.

As individuals we can realise our potential only through belonging to a community. Our contribution to that community is the true measure of our achievement. Some are bound to take longer than others to reach their goals. Whether we become what is in us to become depends on many things. What we possess at birth will develop and flourish, or deteriorate, or become warped, according to the opportunity offered by our environment. Parents and teachers are made more fully aware of the joint nature of their responsibility when their children learn at abnormal rates.

14

The teacher and her job

A person who admits in public to being a teacher is invariably beset by strangers who are anxious to pour out the problems and joys of their offspring: 'This will interest you . . .' or 'Perhaps you'll know what to do about . . .' She is expected to be an authority on nervous disorders, behaviour problems, physical disabilities, intellectual idiosyncrasies, and even marriage and family planning. These skills in fact serve to define the nature of her job.

We could perhaps say that the teacher of young children needs to be a specialist in children. 'Love of children' is not enough and her desire to help them needs the support of academic study of the child and the way in which he develops. She needs to cultivate a clinical detachment towards children and this helps her to understand their problems and sustain them in their efforts, without letting herself become too emotionally involved.

The successful teacher of young children has made herself an authority on children. She needs to know as much about them as any parent or education official. Only then can she assess the findings of people such as Susan Isaacs, or Piaget, or Bernstein, and the value of every new theory or procedure. How else can she estimate the claims made by the promoters of i.t.a., programmed learning, or closed-circuit television?

Reaching out

Those who wish to become Infant teachers are usually people with great insight into children, but intuitive and emotional thinking must be supported by a foundation of knowledge and intellectual understanding.

The image of the Infant School teacher as the mother substitute is gone. The child doesn't need a second mother in school. He has a mother at home and in school he needs to find a person who can challenge him into fresh growth. It is because she is not involved emotionally, as the mother is, that the teacher is able to stimulate intellectual development in the child.

Teachers are bombarded on all sides with advice. Every citizen, from the city councillor and the parent to the bus conductor and the journalist, feels free to offer advice and instruction. More powerful still are the psychologists and other scientists engaged in research who offer fresh theory and evidence in support of it.

The importance of the teacher's professional training is that it enables her to take a more detached and informed view of education than the 'man in the street'. Through her study of educational psychology, sociology, history and philosophy, she learns to understand more fully her own personality and to accept, if only for careful analysis, many ideas to which she was originally hostile. It is made clear to her that the cautious, scientific statements of psychologists or sociologists do not, in themselves, tell her how to handle children. Her own judgement will be called upon in the solution of many of her problems and her decisions will often depend on her personal philosophy or religious faith. A teacher is a person who has learned how to read and evaluate, to write and discuss, and so to become more secure in what she believes. In this way she will develop a sense of conviction. She will know that there are many different forms of organisation, many different methods of education, and she will discover that the research worker may prove to be a most useful ally. Above all she will study, and

The teacher and her job

continue to study, her children so that in the words of the Plowden Report she may 'bring to bear on [her] day-to-day problems astringent intellectual scrutiny' (Par. 550).

A teacher also needs to face the fact that the job she has chosen will confront her perpetually with problems she cannot solve. She does what she can, but she doesn't feel guilty when she fails. Those whose job involves them so essentially in the human situation cannot expect to solve all the problems presented by people. In spite of all a teacher has learned about child development she will constantly come up against behaviour she cannot explain and disappointments she cannot rectify.

Education for a professional job should make a person articulate about her work. Amongst the many things expected of a teacher is the ability to explain to others what her job is about. She should be able to tell parents how children learn to read in a modern classroom, to express her educational beliefs to HMIs or Directors of Education, to explain why she needs a piece of equipment, or to describe her work and ideas to students in training. And if she is to do these things successfully she must carry in her mind a map of her own profession, so that she can show how what she is doing in the Infant School fits into the total pattern of the child's education. It is no use, for instance, eulogising about the discovery approach to learning unless she has a clear idea as to how the work the child does in the Infant School can develop at the later stages. Her study of children must extend to the years of adolescence.

The function of the teacher in the Infant School was the topic of extensive research led by Dorothy Gardner and Joan Cass. The results of this research are published in *The Role of the Teacher in the Infant and Nursery School*, and the way in which these teachers are working is very clearly described.[36] A study of this work reveals the very challenging nature of the teacher's job. Teaching at any stage is a challenge to the teacher's personality, and this is particularly true at the primary stages where personality development is still very immature.

Only the mature personality is secure enough to encourage individuality in others. Some teachers, for instance, find the gifted child a threat to themselves as less gifted persons. A shy person may resent the social success of a child and squash him because he is 'precocious'. Some, as we have seen, wish to dominate and use the child to fulfil themselves, rather than help him to become himself. An individual must feel firmly established in his own individuality before he can regard others as separate individuals in their own right. A sign of personal maturity is the ability to make a mature relationship, or one in which each person helps to affirm the personality of the other.[37]

The quality of relationships which exist in a teacher's class are in many ways a reflection of her own person, and immaturities in herself tend to exaggerate similar immaturities in children. We tend to emphasise in the behaviour of the young what we are ourselves. For this reason, if for no other, the younger the child, the greater is his need for contact with a mature person in his teacher. The young probationer *can* be a mature person, but as a rule she has much to learn before she can meet the demands made on her person by the very young, and a class consisting entirely of new entrants may be more than she can cope with.

However confident a teacher may be in the educational opportunities she provides for her children, she needs to know that each child is making the best possible use of his environment and that he is making progress. It is easy to forget the quiet child who causes her no inconvenience; it is difficult to stretch the gifted child. Careful individual records are essential, particularly where the children work on individual lines.

Some local authorities still insist on the use of uniform record cards, or even record books, but most Infant Schools are left responsible for designing their own methods of record-keeping. Each teacher will work out her own way of doing this, and her records should include:

(1) A class diary indicating major developments in the class

in relation to the rest of the school. This diary will carry over from day to day, with notes on how activities will be followed up, when to introduce further material, when fresh sources of stimulation should be introduced, etc. From time to time the teacher can review what is happening, while looking ahead and anticipating further developments.

(2) A record for each child, indicating, with dates, significant features in his development. It is helpful for the teacher to keep a desk jotter to make a quick note of incidents as they occur, entering them against the child's name at the end of the day; otherwise much is forgotten. If the entries are dated, they present a general picture of the child's rate of progress. Sometimes the very appearance of a page in such records is significant. A great number of entries may indicate that a child is demanding too much attention for some reason; very few entries may mean that a child is withdrawn, apathetic, or physically below par.

The main value of these records is the guidance they give to the teacher who writes them. It may be inadvisable to pass on the records from teacher to teacher or from school to school, as children respond in different ways to different situations and people, and each fresh relationship should start from scratch. On the other hand these records can be useful once a new relationship is established. In many schools head teachers keep records of developments throughout the school as a whole. Careful observation of experiences, linked with accurate recording, constitutes the scientific study of the job. From these recordings theory emerges and in this way the philosophy of the school is established. Indeed the major part of this study of *Young Children Learning* is a development of the records kept by the author during her fifteen years' experience as a headmistress in Infant and Infant/Junior Schools.

The view a teacher takes of her job depends on the view she takes of childhood and the part childhood plays in the process of human development. What she feels about education stems from her basic assumptions regarding human nature and the philosophy she has found for herself as a person gifted with life. If the work done by teachers and children is to have meaning and purpose it must have direction. The purpose we find for education is the purpose we find for living. It is not so much a question of working with an end-product in view as of growing in faith – a faith that the fullest use of the moment will ultimately bring to us the full development of the person within the life he is given.

How can a teacher measure success in her job? Is it through the recognition she gains from other people, the achievement of promotion, or the claims she can make for the accomplishments of her pupils? How does she know that her job is worth while?

One can meet the successful teacher at every level: as a University professor expounding the wonder of nuclear physics, as the head teacher of a Comprehensive School rejoicing in the late developer, as the teacher in a tiny one-class country school serving the village community in a variety of ways. Successful teachers have one quality in common: the sheer joy derived from the job they are doing.

The teacher's job is by no means a perpetually joyful experience, yet it should offer us from time to time the ultimate joy of knowing that we have played an essential part in the growth of a person. Sometimes this comes to us when things are going well, but more often our joy is found in the job's most distressing moments. There is little to compare with the first happy smile of a child who has developed anti-social behaviour in a socially deprived home, or the sight of a child of limited interests caught up in the wonder of the crystal rock in the teacher's display. These are moments when the teacher knows that a door has been opened in the child's life. It is these moments which make the teacher's job one of the most demanding and rewarding of experiences.

Suggestions for further reading

Chapter 1

1 A number of American books show the extent of this research, e.g.
   (a) **Carmichael, L.** (Ed.) *Manual of Child Psychology.* Wiley, 1954.
   (b) **Hurlock, E. B.** *Child Development.* McGraw-Hill, 1950.
2 **McGraw, M.** *The Neuro-Muscular Maturation of the Human Infant.* Columbia University Press, 1943.
3 **Peters, R. S.** *The Concept of Motivation.* London: Routledge, 1958.

Chapter 2

4 (a) **Gesell, A.** and **Ilg, F. L.** *An Introduction to the Study of Human Growth.* Harper, 1949.
   (b) **Gesell, A.** *Studies in Child Development.* Harper, 1948.
   (c) **Munn, N. L.** *Psychology* (Part Two). Harrap, 1961.
5 **Valentine, C. W.** *Parents and Children. A First Book on the Psychology of Child Development and Training.* Methuen, 1953.
6 **Halsey, A. H., Floud, J.,** and **Arnold Anderson, C.** *Education, Economy and Society* (Part Four). Collier-Macmillan, 1961.

7 **Cooper, G. E.** *The Place of Play in an Infant and Junior School.* National Froebel Foundation (London), 1958.
8 **Slade, P.** *Child Drama.* ULP, 1954.

Chapter 3

9 (a) **Luria, A. R.** and **Yudovich, F.** *Speech and the Development of Mental Processes in the Child.* Staples Press, 1959.
  (b) **Lewis, M. M.** *How Children Learn to Speak.* Harrap, 1957.
10 **Grey, Walter W.** *The Living Brain* (page 73). Penguin, 1961. (See also **McGraw,** No. 2 above.)
11 **Whitehead, A. N.** *The Aims of Education and Other Essays.* Williams and Norgate, 1929.
12 (a) **Hebb, D. O.** *The Organisation of Behaviour.* Wiley, 1949.
  (b) **Munn, N. L.** *The Evolution and Growth of Human Behaviour.* Houghton Mifflin, 1955.
13 **Gesell, A.** and **Ilg, F. L.** *The Child from Five to Ten.* Harper, 1946.
14 (a) **Isaacs, N.** and **Theakston, T. R.** *Some Aspects of Piaget's Work.* National Froebel Foundation (London), 1955.
  (b) **Lovell, K.** *The Growth of Basic Mathematical and Scientific Concepts in Children.* ULP, 1961.

Chapter 4

15 (a) **Tanner, J. M.** *Education and Physical Growth.* ULP, 1961.
  (b) **Gesell, A.** (See Nos. 4(a), 4(b), and 13 above.)
16 See **Munn** (No. 4(c) above), Chapter 7 in the Fourth Edition.
17 **Flemming, C. M.** *Adolescence: its Social Psychology.* Routledge and Kegan Paul, 1955.
18 (a) **Ash, B.** and **Rapaport, B.** *Creative Work in the Junior School.* Methuen, 1957.
  (b) **Ash, B.** and **Rapaport, B.** *The Junior School Today.* National Froebel Foundation (London), 1958.

Suggestions for further reading

19 *Children and Their Primary Schools* (The Plowden Report), Volume 1 (Chapter 10). HMSO, 1967.
20 (a) **Glynn, D.** *Teach Your Child to Read.* Pearson, 1964.
   (b) **Walters, Elsa H.** *Activity and Experience in the Infant School.* National Froebel Foundation (London), 1951.

Chapter 5

21 (a) *Children and Their Primary Schools*, Paragraphs 65, 74. (See No. 19 above).
   (b) **Hurlock, E. B.** *Developmental Psychology.* McGraw-Hill, 1959.
   (c) **Gesell, A.** et al. *The First Five Years of Life.* Harper, 1940.
22 **Carter, C. O.** *Human Heredity.* Penguin, 1962.
23 (a) **Wiseman, S.** *Education and Environment.* Manchester University Press, 1964.
   (b) **Douglas, J. W. B.** *The Home and the School.* MacGibbon and Kee, 1964.

Chapter 11

24 See the Plowden Report (No. 19, above), Chapters 9 and 10.
25 (a) **Frazer, E.** *Home Environment and the School.* ULP, 1959.
   (b) **James, H. E. O.** et al. *Periods of Stress in the Primary School.* National Association for Mental Health, 1956.
   (c) **Valentine, C. W.** (See No. 5 above.)

Chapter 12

26 (a) **Bowlby, J.** *Maternal Care and Mental Health.* Geneva WHO, 1951.
   (b) **Lewis, M. M.** *Language, Thought and Personality in Infancy and Childhood.* Harrap, 1963.

27 (a) **Gardner, D. E. M.** *The Education of Young Children.* Methuen, 1956.
   (b) **Isaacs, Susan.** *The Children We Teach.* ULP, 1937.
28 (a) **Catty, N.** *Learning and Teaching in the Junior School.* Methuen, 1956.
   (b) **Garrison, K.** *Growth and Development.* Longmans, 1952.

Chapter 13

29 **Allport, G. W.** *Pattern and Growth in Personality.* Holt, Rinehart and Winston, 1963.

30 **Miller, G. A.** *The Science of Mental Life.* Pelican (Penguin), 1966.
   A comprehensive survey of some of the leading psychologists in the last hundred years or so, with a chapter on Binet.

31 **Shields, R. W.** *A Cure of Delinquents: the Treatment of Maladjustment.* Heinemann, 1962.

32 **Penrose, L. S.** *Biology of Mental Defect.* Sidgwick & Jackson, 1964.

33 **Branch, M.** and **Cash, A.** *Gifted Children.* Souvenir Press, 1966. For anoxia see Chapter 19, 'The Decompression Experiment'.

34 **Bowlby, John.** *Child Care and the Growth of Love.* Pelican (Penguin), 1966.
   Based, by permission of the World Health Organisation, on the report *Maternal Care and Mental Health* by J. Bowlby.

35 **Bernstein, B.** *Social Class and Linguistic Development: a Theory of Social Learning.*
   From *Education, Economy and Society.* Ed. Halsey, A. H. *et al.* (See No. 6.)

Chapter 14

36 **Gardner, D. E. M.** and **Cass, J. E.** *The Role of the Teacher in the Infant and Nursery School.* Pergamon Press, 1965.

37 (a) **Overstreet, H. A.** *The Mature Mind.* Gollancz, 1939.
   (b) **Storr, A.** *The Integrity of the Personality.* Pelican (Penguin), 1964.

Suggestions for further reading

Additional reading for Chapter 13

Clarke, A. M. and **Clark, A. D. B.** *Mental Deficiency. The Changing Outlook* (Manuals of Modern Psychology). Methuen, 1958.
An interesting review of our changing and more enlightened attitude to mental deficiency.

Douglas, J. W. B. *The Home and the School.* MacGibbon and Kee, 1964.
A study of ability and attainment in the primary school, with an introduction by Professor D. V. Glass.

Getzels, J. W. and **Jackson, P. W.** *Creativity and Intelligence.* Wiley, 1962.

Hebb, D. O. *The Organisation of Behaviour.* Wiley, 1949.

Illingworth, R. S. *The Normal School Child and His Problems, Physical and Emotional.* Heinemann, 1964.

Lorenz, C. *King Solomon's Ring* (New light on animal ways), translated by Marjorie Keir Wilson. Methuen, 1952.
Delightfully illustrated by margin drawings. (Now also a paper-back.)

Newsom Report. *Half Our Future.* HMSO, 1963.
A report of the Central Advisory Council for Education (England) on the education of pupils aged 13 to 16 of average and less than average ability.

Nunn, Sir Percy. *Education, Its Data and First Principles.* Edward Arnold, 3rd Edn. 1945.

Schonell, F. *Backwardness in the Basic Subjects.* Oliver & Boyd, 1959.
A basic book for all interested in backward children from an educational point of view.

Tanner, J. M. *Education and Physical Growth.* ULP, 1961.
Implications of the child's physical growth for educational theory and practice.

Tansley, A. F. and **Gulliford, R.** *The Education of Slow-learning Children.* Routledge and Kegan Paul, 1961 (Paper-back 1966).
A book which skilfully combines theory and practice in the education of the slow-learning child.

Index

adjustment, in infancy 16; to school 15
aesthetic interests 60
baby, completeness of 25; dependency of 17; new-born 13-14
behaviour, modes of 18; patterns 13; problems 87
books 60
bricks 56
child, acceptance of 85; curiosity of 59; nature of 12
childhood, nature of 26; timelessness of 68
children with special gifts 98-100
classroom, organisation 72-4; present-day practice in 11
development, stages in 30-2; total nature of 25
discipline 86
education, child-centred 42 48 53; patterns of State 32-3
entry to school 84
environment, balanced 54; heredity and 31 35; outdoor 60
equipment, purpose of 56
fighting 19
freedom 86
grouping, vertical 61-4 74
growth, continuity of 32; critical periods in 33; stages in 31
home, and school 68 77-83
individuality, accepting the child's 39; at five years old 30 36; how children differ 37-8; spiritual significance of 40 41
Infant and Junior School relationships 66
intelligence 92-3; tests 92
learning: comparison of learning situations 52; continuity in 28; in the home 18; informal learning in school 49; integration in 27; interrelated nature of 26; readiness to learn 34; social 19; sources of 55; spontaneous 53; urge to learn 13
materials, exploring 22; man's 57; waste 58
mathematical exploration 59
milk in school 60
name, child's 40
need, for recognition 41; varied needs of children 55
organisation, of classroom 72; of school 65
parents, co-operation of 78; incidental relationships with 81; parent-teacher relationships 78-80
personality, part played by learning 42; pattern 43; school contribution to 45; value of 42
personal relationships, importance of 44
play, as a guide to the child 24; domestic 56; dramatic 59; exploring through 21; purpose of 20; social 22; types of 23
playtime breaks 71
Plowden Report 33 65-6 80-1 103
school, use of whole 73
self, child's idea of 73
sense organs, function of 26
slow learner 89-90 94-7
teacher, as a specialist in children 101; influence of 54; in society 101; personality of 103-4; problems of 103; records of 104-5; role in mental health of child 84-7 90; successfulness of 106; teamwork 65; view of her job 106
understanding, growth of 28-9
writing 58